Breaking Out of the Box: Interdisciplinary Collaboration and Faculty Work

Breaking Out of the Box: Interdisciplinary Collaboration and Faculty Work

by

Marilyn J. Amey and Dennis F. Brown

Michigan State University

INFORMATION AGE
PUBLISHING

80 Mason Street • Greenwich, Connecticut 06830 • www.infoagepub.com

Library of Congress Cataloging-in-Publication Data

Amey, Marilyn J.
 Breaking out of the box : interdisciplinary collaboration and faculty
work / by Marilyn J. Amey and Dennis F. Brown.
   p. cm.
 Includes bibliographical references and index.
 ISBN 1-59311-132-0 (pbk.) — ISBN 1-59311-133-9 (hardcover)
 1. Interdisciplinary approach in education. 2. Universities and
colleges—Departments. 3. Interdisciplinary research. 4. College
teachers—Professional relationships. I. Brown, Dennis F. II. Title.
 LB2360.2.A44 2004
 378.1'2—dc22

                                                    2004020282

Printed in the United States of America

CONTENTS

List of Tables

To Caitlin and Megan for your patience, your endless support, and your inspiration in opening the box. We hope to always help you break out of the boxes and continue to be your creative, unique selves.

PREFACE

When our daughter was 4 years old, she began to watch a Saturday morning children's show entitled, "Out of the Box." Although we thought it was an odd name for a children's program, the title aptly described the primary objective of the show: to help children be creative and use their imaginations. The children on the show each day picked items out of a large box and then created an impromptu story, made musical instruments and craft projects, and learned to think from the perspectives of one of the other children on the show. In reality, the program was scripted, but to a 4-year-old, the "made-up" story and other activities each day gave her license to be original and creative.

There is little question that most universities with a research mission are organized specifically to discover or create new knowledge. This function is organized around the disciplinary nature of departments. In a sense, the university, through its departmental organization and faculty culture is scripted to think within disciplinary boxes. Faculties are organized by discipline, disseminate research through discipline-based journals and conferences, and are rewarded for contributing to and expanding the disciplinary knowledge base. The next generation of faculty are trained and enculturated into their specific disciplinary model during graduate school and early career experiences, thus perpetuating and scripting future faculty in the disciplinary lens. Each generation of new faculty are encouraged to be original and creative while maintaining strict methodological integrity. One feels the press to become a national expert in a particular subject area, which comes from publishing frequently in top-tier journals in the field. The broad knowledge of graduate education quickly morphs to individual specializations, and the most successful route to advancement for faculty appears to be staying close to the intellectual vest of the discipline. We are not often taught or rewarded for thinking "out of the box," but rather for continuing to focus within the disciplinary box. We believe that faculty can think creatively and apart from their disciplinary traditions, "out of the box" so to speak, and that interdisciplinary collaboration is a means to help faculty make this transition.

We are not alone in these thoughts, of course, but also did not come of our views quickly. They emerged through the close examination of a specific research team we were independently hired to study. Although we had worked together previously on research projects, we had never studied interdisciplinary collaboration nor had we ever participated on equal footing in a research project. So the experiences recounted in this text not only come from those we recorded from the research team we studied for an extended period of time but also from the thoughts gleaned from our own experiences as an "interdisciplinary pair" asked to conduct this study. In many ways, we lived the model we were studying and were not always any more conscious of the transition processes in which we were engaged than the members of the team we studied.

We were asked separately to be involved with this project because of our individual expertise and spent over a year between the two of us connected to it. One of us studies leadership and faculty work, with disciplinary training in education and public administration. The other worked in social services for years before transitioning into higher education administration and brought disciplinary lenses from sociology, organizational behavior, and organizational development to the project. One has spent years publishing qualitative research and the other, writing administrative memos and executive summaries. We have spent over 3 years culling the data, sharing our findings, thinking and rethinking those lessons we learned, and trying to decide of what use we think they are to higher education and faculty work. The potential for failure, cognitive clashes, positional posturing, and different work and writing styles did not have the same professional consequences for us as they did for members of the research team. Yet, we were affected quite similarly by the same transitions in disciplinary orientation, knowledge engagement, and work orientation we saw emerge in the behaviors of research team members.

Particularly striking to us in retrospect, has been the ways in which we moved through our own paradigm explorations, how we have had to really listen and learn that the other's perspectives might be as relevant (or more so) in understanding what we were seeing, and to find a common language through which we could tell the stories of our research team. We began the project as faculty do—exercising our independence as experts, carving up the tasks and going about our work independently.

What we found was not unexpected. The pieces of the puzzle did not fit together always nor was there a single voice, or even an integrated one. To move beyond the "yours and mine" phase of understanding the interdisciplinary collaboration experience of the research team, we too had to find the intellectual neutral space that afforded us opportunity to pause and reflect. We had to let go of our subconscious positional bargaining stances where we tried to force ideas into one paradigm or another. We had to develop deeper cognitive understandings of each other's perspectives, which required far more time, listening, and discussion than two people who have worked together over 15 years expect to spend. We have had to negotiate with ourselves and our work units time spent on this effort, outlets for dissemination, and the legitimacy of co-authored work, facing much the same challenges as those we depict in the text. The learning odyssey has been amazing, frustrating, slow, intellectually growthful, and a more authentic accounting of the data we gathered than either of us could have done had we stayed in our expert thinking mode.

This book is not solely about interdisciplinary collaboration, team building or team development. Certainly many of these aspects have influenced the development of our interdisciplinary collaboration model. Yet, our focus in this text is on the significant cognitive changes faculty experience during interdisciplinary collaborations as well as their orientation toward group work, and how they apply their expert disciplinary knowledge when working with faculty from other disciplines. The end product, hopefully, is a new approach to old complex problems and perhaps, the creation of new knowledge. It certainly has been a new approach for us and has resulted in new ways each of us thinks about faculty work and interdisciplinary collaboration.

We have many colleagues to thank for their patience and support throughout this project; they know who they are. They gave us feedback, talked us through our ideas, challenged us to see things more deeply, and continued to believe we could finish this book. We want especially to thank Lorilee Sandmann, who hired each of us to work on the project originally, starting us down this path, Philip Altbach for his patience and guidance, and the folks at our favorite coffee shop where we spent countless hours writing, discussing, and collaborating.

CHAPTER 1

INTRODUCTION

In the complex arena of postsecondary education, we hear calls for increased interdisciplinary collaboration. "Because knowledge arises within social contexts and in multiple forms, the key to increasing knowledge lies in the effort to extend one's limited perspective" (Bartlett, 1990, p. 882, cited in Bensimon & Neumann, 1993). Critics suggest cross-unit relationships and multidisciplinary thinking are required to address the kinds of problems facing higher education into the future, implying that the more narrow lenses of single disciplinary orientations do not fully lend themselves to complex issues. Unfortunately, critics do not provide as much insight into how such collaborative arrangements are developed or sustained. Despite an impressive accumulation of experience and case study, it remains unclear which variables are most likely to produce success in collaborations (Sandmann & Flynn, 1997). What is known is that organizational/unit functioning, culture, norms, values and reward structures significantly impact what faculty work gets done, the designs through which work is accomplished, and who participates (Blackburn & Lawrence, 1995; Bolman & Deal, 1997; Fairweather, 1996; Mattesich & Monsey, 1992; Oborn & Shipley, 1995; Trubowitz & Longo, 1997). It is less clear how universities more effectively cultivate and support interdisciplinary collaboration or the process through which faculty and staff travel in enacting this form of work. Leadership skills required for interdisciplinary groups are also not well understood.

An ideal model and process would successfully integrate competing perspectives, develop a shared sense of power and change among all par-

Breaking Out of the Box: Interdisciplinary Collaboration and Faculty Work, 1–15
Copyright © 2004 by Information Age Publishing

ticipants, and demonstrate a leadership role that was well-defined and replicable (Sandmann & Flynn, 1997). In actuality, work we call interdisciplinary collaborative processes is most often characterized by dominance of a single disciplinary change paradigm, mixed perceptions of improvement or goal attainment, and poorly resolved group tension. We began this project in an effort to capture and develop a more accurate sense of interdisciplinary collaboration such as the ideal Sandmann and Flynn envisioned.

WHAT IS INTERDISCIPLINARY COLLABORATION?

We conceive of interdisciplinary collaboration as a group of faculty and staff from various disciplinary backgrounds (paradigms), often within a single university, organized to address a predetermined task. The starting place of this multiple disciplinary effort is to purposely bring together members from various fields to apply their expertise in successfully resolving complex problems. Unlike traditional faculty work, the intent is to have the faculty come together intellectually. The purpose is for faculty to think collectively in generating strategies that utilize the strengths of their individual expertise in a more genuinely integrated way.

Interdisciplinary collaboration efforts are risky for a number of reasons that will be discussed more in depth later in this book. But a primary risk of assembling faculty from various disciplinary perspectives is the potential, or should we say, probability, that disciplinary clashes will ultimately disrupt the collaborative process of the group and hence, sabotage the effectiveness of the group to create the new solutions. So facilitating this kind of work may require different forms of leadership than we typically see in heads of committees or department chairs. We believe that interdisciplinary collaboration affords faculty an opportunity to learn from each other and foster new ways of thinking resulting in the creation of new knowledge within and, potentially, apart from the group itself. The potential for the institution of new knowledge far outweighs the potential risks involved.

WHY IS INTERDISCIPLINARY COLLABORATION IMPORTANT?

As stated above, we believe that multiple perspectives can better resolve complex problems as opposed to singular disciplinary based solutions, and we are not alone in believing this (e.g., Austin & Baldwin, 1991; Bennis, 1997; Bensimon & Neumann, 1993; Gray, 1989; Klein, 1990; Salter & Hearn, 1996; Sandmann & Flynn, 1987). Multiple perspectives vastly improve the chance for creative solutions to problems as opposed to solutions resulting from a singular disciplinary perspective. Interdisciplinary collaboration affords the opportunity for the group to view and interpret problems in new ways, which leads to the creation of new approaches to problems and problem solving. The adage, "two heads are better than one" is an oversimplification of the point. But it is true that those who value interdisciplinarity believe that multiple perspectives are required to address complex problems. So it becomes not only are two heads needed, but two (or more) heads that see the world through different lenses are required. Members of the group learn from each other's perspectives because those viewpoints are respected and can be shared, perhaps even internalized. Through dialogue, members find other ways of making sense of the world that complement their disciplinary perspectives rather than contradict them. In learning from each other, original beliefs are appropriately challenged, reflection occurs, and more informed and often, changed perspectives emerge. Interdisciplinary collaboration fosters new ways of thinking as members move from thinking strictly from their disciplinary perspective to blending their perspectives and thinking integratively.

Instead of looking for contradictions or holes in other disciplinary paradigms for the purpose of argument and co-option, members may become more aware of the weak areas of their own intellectual orientations and see the strengths of other disciplinary perspectives. As a result, new ideas that complement their own perspective are incorporated. Differences in thought are not minimized in value or ignored because of the power and group status of others. They are heard, considered, and honored for what new insights they bring to the forefront. This group process may result in a cognitive shift for some but not all of the members. We do not propose this approach to faculty work as a panacea for intellectual growth and development. But we found the process of engagement in interdisciplinary collaboration far more potentially fruitful in creating intellectual change than is often the case in other, differently structured "team" activities.

Faculty and staff also experience a new or different way of working with each other. Instead of working individually on their own piece of the project, as is often the way project components get allocated, members learn to engage collaboratively as a team. To do so, they have to learn from each other. Faculty feel a collective ownership for the direction of the team, the strategies they develop, the decisions they make, and the outcomes of their work. They feed off each other's enthusiasm and successes. The team members see the holistic perspective of the project rather than an isolated piece. Critiques of individual member tasks and contributions by other members of the group are accepted rather than perceived to be threatening and rebuffed. Clearly, working as a team is a critical part in the evolution of an interdisciplinary collaboration.

INTERDISCIPLINARITY

Before we introduce our interdisciplinary collaboration model, it is useful to discuss two concepts we feel are extremely important to the understanding of our model. The two concepts are interdisciplinarity and collaboration. These terms have been used widely and interchangeably with others in the research literature and in practice. Our use of the terms is very purposeful and specific.

What Do We Mean By Interdisciplinary?

While it might appear easy to define interdisciplinary, the literature seems to present a blurred definition and certainly an absence of consensus on a definition. This is due primarily to the fact that the term interdisciplinarity has been applied to a wide range of contexts, each representing different situations and intended outcomes. For example, the term was used to describe efforts to create a new discipline from two other disciplines. It also is a label used when groups from different disciplines are organized to address a single predetermined problem from multiple perspectives. Depending in which situation the term is being applied, the meaning of interdisciplinarity can vary greatly.

Given the wide range of research activity associated with the term interdisciplinarity, Salter and Hearn (1996) have divided the literature into two camps. One camp, labeled "instrumental" interdisciplinarity deals with the integration of existing frameworks (i.e., disciplinary perspectives) into a temporary synthesis based on a specific problem (p. 29-30). Often referred to as applied research or problem-based research, instrumental interdisciplinarity seeks a unity of practice that is temporary and based solely on a particular situation or problem. While new knowledge can be created from instrumental interdisciplinary efforts, it has no disciplinary home, no epistemology, or method to attach to. The instrumental interdisciplinary literature provides the concept closest to the situation of the research team on which our model is based.

Salter and Hearn (1996) also suggest a second camp of interdisciplinary activity labeled "conceptual" interdisciplinarity. Researchers coming from this perspective are more concerned with epistemological issues than problem based. Work in the conceptual interdisciplinary arena seeks a unity of knowledge that is permanent and serves as a foundation for a new and legitimate discipline. In this camp, new knowledge is understood to be transformative.

There are a number of terms associated with interdisciplinarity that have also been used to explain or describe this concept. These terms include multidisciplinarity and transdisciplinarity. Again, the use of these terms has been situation specific but it is worthwhile to briefly note the usage here. Klein's (1990) work helped us distinguish these terms in an attempt to dispel their misuse, or at least their multiple uses. Klein writes,

> Most purportedly "interdisciplinary" activities are not "interdisciplinary" but "multidisciplinary" or "pluraldisciplinary." "Multidisciplinarity" signifies the juxtaposition of disciplines. It is essentially additive, not integrative. Even in a common environment, educators, researchers and practitioners still behave as disciplinarians with different perspectives. Their relationship may be mutual and cumulative but not interactive, for there is "no apparent connection," no real cooperation, or "explicit" relationship, and even perhaps, a "questionable eclecticism." The participating disciplines are neither changed nor enriched, and the lack of a "well defined matrix" of interactions means disciplinary relationships are likely to be limited and transitory. (p. 56)

Klein's (1990) notions of additive and interactive are key concepts for understanding the differences between multidisciplinarity, interdisciplinarity and transdisciplinarity. She notes that, "interdisciplinarity does not spontaneously emerge by putting an economist and a sociologist, or any other combination of specialist, in close proximity. Nor does an interdisciplinary field reach maturity in just a few decades. An interdisciplinary field constitutes a unique form of specialization. It is a selective integration within a spectrum of disciplines" (p. 116).

In contrast, transdisciplinarity is more comprehensive in scope and vision, suggesting an "overarching synthesis" or framework that transcends the narrower disciplinary world views and breaks the boundaries of one or more disciplines. Perhaps Jantsch (in Klein, 1990, p. 66) provides us with a more clear distinction between these two concepts. Jantsch asserts, "Whereas 'interdisciplinarity' signifies the synthesis of two or more disciplines, establishing a new metalevel discourse, 'transdisciplinarity' signifies the interconnectedness of all aspects of reality, transcending the dynamics, a dialectical synthesis to grasp the total dynamics of reality as a whole."

While we believe that any form of interdisciplinarity has the potential for knowledge creation, our model evolved from the case study of our research team and sits squarely in the "instrumental interdisciplinary" camp where the team was assembled with the purpose of addressing a predetermined problem. The intent was to use the expertise from multiple perspectives to create solutions to a complex set of problems that were not easily or effectively resolved from a single disciplinary perspective. No new interdisciplinary field of knowledge was intended to result from this project, although the project administrator who convened the group had hope for generative thinking among members from the beginning. No theory building or transitive synthesis of disciplines was evident.

In light of this discussion of concepts from the literature, we are still faced with the task of defining interdisciplinarity. Within the conceptual framework of the instrumental or applied research camp, the definition we prefer to use is a modified version of one originally posited by the Center for Educational Research and Innovation. It was also used by Lattuca (2002a) in her recent discussion of "learning interdisciplinarity." Our definition of interdisciplinarity is:

> An adjective describing the interaction among two or more different disciplines. This interaction may range from simple communication of ideas to the mutual integration of organizing concepts, methodology, procedures, epistemology, terminology, data, and organization of research and education in a fairly large field. An interdisciplinary group consists of persons trained in different fields of knowledge (disciplines) with different concepts, methods, and data in terms organized into a common effort on a common problem with continuous intercommunication among the participants from the different disciplines. (Organization for Economic Cooperation and Development, 1972, pp. 25-26)

The second part of the definition reflects the underlying rationale for the structure of the team we observed, so fits our purposes well as written. The first part of the definition, however, is where we would make slight modifications in wording but significant change in meaning. In its simplest form, according to the Organization of Economic Cooperation and Development, interdisciplinary involves an interaction between two or more disciplines. Presumably, this interaction can take place in numerous venues. For example, it might be thought of to characterize what happens between colleagues from different disciplines coteaching a class, to colleagues working together on a research project to coauthoring a book. We do not agree that "simple communication of ideas" represents interdisciplinarity. A mere collection of colleagues from different disciplinary paradigms communicating ideas does not constitute an interdisciplinary group to us. It only means there are multiple disciplines present. There is an absence of any form of integrating perspectives, which we believe is central.

The key is how group members interact with each other and what is the end result. If one of the two interdisciplinary paradigms dominates the work of the colleagues, then in reality there is no interdisciplinary nature to this work. There is only one perspective being enacted between two colleagues who are from different disciplines. Thus, in order for interdisciplinarity to exist, there must be some intellectual interaction between the two disciplinary perspectives. The place on the continuum representing mutual integration is in line with what we have come to call interdisciplinarity. The cognitive interchange, processing, owning and integrating of information is a key distinction between our definition of interdisciplinary and many others. With this definition comes the risk of an ideal not to be accomplished frequently in academe for reasons that become clear throughout this text. Yet, the evolutionary intellectual processes exhibited by our research team support the need for a more integrative learning perspective than the mere information sharing implied in the beginning of the Center for Educational Research and Innovation definition of interdisciplinarity.

At its inception, the group we studied (or any group newly formed) was a collection of faculty and staff representing multiple disciplines. They would not have described themselves as interdisciplinary, and neither would we. As they transitioned through the stages we proposed in our model, the group became a team whose collective cognitive lens was more integrative and possibly transformational. This is when they became interdisciplinary and new knowledge could be created.

An important component of interdisciplinary interaction is that the disciplinary perspectives begin to blend. This suggests that the process of interdisciplinarity is intellectually developmental along a continuum. Members of the group have to begin to change their thinking in some way. Members' disciplinary paradigms come into play with one another as the group attempts to define and discuss the tasks before them. As embedded assumptions are challenged and evolve, so do the solutions and possible knowledge base(s) of the multidisciplinary group. An interdisciplinary group ceases to be a collection of members from various disciplines and begins to be a team in which members engage with and are informed by each other's disciplinary perspectives.

While the discussion of interdisciplinarity focuses on the disciplinary frameworks or paradigms held by each of the group members and the way they view and interpret the world, the second concept of our interdisciplinary model is the concept of collaboration. Collaboration refers to how the members of the group work together.

What Do We Mean By the Concept of Collaboration?

In our use of term collaboration, it is first necessary to draw a distinction with the concepts of coordination and cooperation. The three terms are often used interchangeably (Austin & Baldwin, 1991). But we believe that there are important distinctions when applied to faculty work.

To illustrate the differences in terms, we begin with what we know about collaboration and draw a clear distinction between our use of the term and the more commonly used concept of cooperation. The literature defines collaboration in many ways and from a variety of perspectives. Two perspectives, one organizational and one individual, help demonstrate the complexity of the context in which the definitions reside. From an organizational (structural) perspective, Mattesich and Monsey (1992, p. 7) define collaboration as: "a mutually beneficial and well-defined relationship entered into by two or more organizations to achieve common goals. The relationship includes a commitment to: a definition of mutual relationships and goals; a jointly developed structure and shared responsibility; mutual authority and accountability for successes; and sharing of resources and rewards."

The key points in this definition of collaboration involve a well-defined relationship committed to the goals and structure of the group, and the mutual authority and accountability for the outcomes. These ideas suggest that the group operates beyond the mere coordination of separate efforts or agreement to work together cooperatively. The relationship shows the mutual authority to make decisions. And the group is accountable for its combined outcomes, not just the pieces of the project. It is a collective effort. Organizationally, Doan (1995) characterizes a cooperation model as two organizations that arrive at a common ground, but their efforts do not advance any further. Individuals or organizations can coordinate resources and efforts, yet have no interdependent relationship or responsibility. While they are not synonymous or interchangeable, both coordination and cooperation are necessary elements of collaboration.

In discussing faculty work, Austin and Baldwin (1991) describe collaboration as, "a cooperative endeavor that involves common goals, coordinated effort, and outcomes or products for which the collaborators share responsibility and credit" (p. 5). They distinguish collaboration from cooperation by noting that collaboration is the narrower term. "Collaboration requires a great deal of cooperation, but the final objectives of the two activities differ somewhat. Individuals who cooperate often reach some agreement but proceed individually toward self determined goals. People who collaborate work closely together and share mutual responsibility for their joint endeavor" (p. 4).

Perhaps Tjosvold's (1986) concept of collaboration draws both organizational and individual perspectives on collaboration closer together. Tjosvold suggests that collaboration is, "a special case of positive interdependence ... of designing contexts and interactive processes in a highly conscious fashion to promote interdependence" (p. 65). Elements of structural relationships (e.g., task/goal interdependence, role definitions, organizational culture rewards, systems of accountability and conflict resolution) and psychological aspects (e.g., individual beliefs, values assumptions and styles) must be taken into account. In our concept of collaboration, both the individual and organizational perspectives are equally important.

There are many examples of joint work that come quickly to mind in the academy that we might alternately call cooperation, coordination or collaboration, although we want to move away from the casual interchange of these terms and draw clearer distinctions in practice. Faculty often work together under the term collaboration but accomplish their work independently in separate pieces or tasks. The last phase of this definition of "collaboration" involves bringing the individual pieces together for a finished product. This common "divide and conquer" strategy is reflective of many aspects of the academy—task forces, research projects, student group projects, curriculum reform, and so forth.

Dividing a group task into pieces for each member to complete can involve coordination of individual efforts or cooperative activity of the group members to complete defined tasks. Often, coauthors in different geographic areas of the country or around the world will complete their parts of a book and share them when putting together the finished product. "You write that piece, I will write this piece, and we will put them together in a book"—much the same as an edited text but without necessarily calling it so. Similarly, research and even class instruction cotaught by two instructors are often labeled collaboration when in fact they are coordinated and/or cooperative efforts. In each case, the finished product is broken down into separate pieces for the individual faculty members to complete. It is not that those involved are not collegial with each other or *collaborative*. But no interactive, deep learning is going on between the participants (Mezirow and Associates, 1990; Mezirow, 1991). Their focus is on completing the tasks and the end product. The rationale for participating is bringing to bear one's expertise for completing a conjoined assignment. The purpose is not to necessarily engage in transformative intellectual growth and development around core beliefs and values. We propose that this more common and basic type of academic activity is one of coordination or cooperation rather than collaboration.

Our definition of collaboration includes a cognitive component of integrated thinking spawned through active listening, dialogue, and learning with/from other members. Perceptions of intellectual equity among members result from and feed back into collaboration in this model. The team, intellectually, is more than the sum of its parts. At the same time, using the holographic metaphor (Morgan, 1999), each member is imbued, at least to some extent, with understandings from others' perspectives.

Under our concept of collaboration, we envision a mutual teaching-learning (give and take) process among the group members where all work on the same task and learn from the discussion with each other regarding the task. Collaboration is integrative, involving the collective cognition of the group. Collaboration is not individualistic or isolated. Collaboration does not hold a dominant perspective. Hopefully, new group orientations are created from the critical examination of old individual perspectives in tandem with the exploration of new ideas.

Characteristics of Collaboration

The literature is replete with the characteristics of successful collaborations, in the academy or in other sectors. Most writers would agree that a successful collaboration requires trust, mutual respect, shared vision, time, open and frequent communication, and flexibility (Mattesich & Monsey, 1992; Oborn & Shipley, 1995; Trubowitz & Longo 1997). Collaborations require a lot of time to develop and deliver (Doan, 1995, Krasnow, 1997). Collaboration must be seen as an investment—beyond the mere completion of a required set of tasks. Members of the collaborative must develop trust and respect for each other in order to foster an atmosphere of honest communication and risk taking in sharing innovative ideas. Collaborations need a strong convener, a leader who helps to set the vision, goals, roles, tasks, and so forth, of the members and nurture the group until an interdependent relationship emerges.

Communication is another key to successful collaborations. Members must be able to communicate constantly (or at least frequently), honestly and with respect throughout the collaboration. Active listening is a skill that the membership must have in a successful collaboration. Members of a collaborative must learn to listen and listen to learn (Krasnow, 1997), which almost seems a trite observation in an educational organization. Too often group members listen to confirm their beliefs and to take issue with ideas that contradict those beliefs. They pause to reload, not to listen. This may be particularly true for faculty whose identity is characterized by their knowledge expertise. Members in a successful collaboration listen to learn, to make connections complementing their own belief system with the ideas that other members are expressing, and to deeply consider ideas that challenge their perspectives and strong convictions.

Perhaps the most important characteristics of a successful collaboration are the attributes and qualities that each member brings to the group. Pick the right people to participate in the collaboration (Mattesich & Monsey, 1992), or "great group" as Bennis calls it (1997), and your chances to succeed increase. What we have learned is that in interdisciplinary collaboration, "right" may be defined differently.

In summary, we envision interdisciplinary collaboration as integrative thinking among participants where new knowledge is created from the interweaving of multiple perspectives. Members of the interdisciplinary collaboration feel ownership for the team, its direction and decision making, and feel accountability to each other. Participants in an interdisciplinary collaboration are motivated by the collegial discourse and learning opportunities leading to the creation of solutions to the task they are working on and new knowledge. These attributes, then, become important parts of the definition of a "right" person to participate in such a collaborative effort.

If we combine the concepts from the discussions of interdisciplinarity and of collaborations, we have the basic tenets of our concept of interdisciplinary collaboration in problem based or applied research. This is the basis for our model summarized below.

THE STUDY OF INTERDISCIPLINARY COLLABORATION

Our thinking is based on results of an intensive study of a university research team, extensive review of the literature, and decades of experiences working in postsecondary institutions.[1] The team represented in this case, which we refer to as our research team, was involved in an 18-month, university-community-agency partnership. The 10-member university team was contracted to provide technical assistance and training to an inner city community council. Our research efforts focused on the processes of interaction among the university team members who represented five different units on campus.

We examined the ways in which university team members developed and enacted an interdisciplinary team and the leadership issues associated with group cohesion. From this analysis, several themes emerged and an interdisciplinary collaboration model was developed to capture the complexity of the activity. Specifically, we examined the consequences for group processes, goal definition, and intervention strategies when competing paradigms exist, the leadership issues that were present, and the degree of impact of the university's culture on successful interdisciplinary collaboration development.

Throughout the study period, it was evident that not only were the group members learning to work together as a team but that the team was learning to work in a very different kind of partnership process. The literature on leadership, teamwork and collaboration suggested evolution would take place, but not necessarily the timeframe or nature of that change. After review of the data, we originally posited the evolution of the team along three dimensions. There are three stages that represent distinctive characteristics along each of the three dimensions of: *discipline orientation, knowledge engagement,* and *work orientation.* Later, after further analysis, we posited a fourth dimension of *leadership orientation.*

The first dimension is the disciplinary orientation continuum. Disciplinary orientation refers to the discipline paradigm that guides how members view and interpret the environment and how they typically address solutions to problems in that environment. There are several approaches to cross-disciplinary work including: dominant, where one paradigm dominates and provides direction and meaning for change; parallel, with paradigms positioned more equally, and different paradigms providing direction and meaning for distinct portions of work without one approach framing the effort; and integrated, where multiple frameworks inform the process, blending together to form an interdisciplinary paradigm. In this final stage, the group is able to integrate the paradigms into a new hybrid, borrowing and combining the most appropriate aspects of each of the disciplinary paradigms. The hybrid or integrative side of the continuum represents a melding of philosophical thought and interdisciplinary learning.

The second dimension is the knowledge engagement continuum. Knowledge engagement refers to how members use discipline knowledge and the role they play within the team. The first stage of knowledge engagement begins with the expert model, moves to the coordinated approach, and finally evolves into a collaborative stage. Traditional outreach and consulting work are examples of the expert model of knowledge engagement. Individuals are sought for their disciplinary expertise and interactions take on almost a "sage on the stage" aura. As development occurs across the continuum, the expert moves to more of a learning facilitator, sharing the intellectual platform with various collaborators, including the clients (Doan, 1995; O'Looney, 1994), and promoting diverse perspectives.

The third dimension is the work orientation and refers to how each member works with other group members. Work orientation begins with a focus on the individual and individual activity, moves through a group orientation, and finally evolves to a team functioning with collective responsibility for goal attainment. The fourth dimension, leadership, refers to the behaviors of the person administratively responsible for group and its contract. Transitions on the leadership dimension were characterized as top-down, facilitative and more inclusive, and finally, web-like or servant.

Table 1.1 depicts a visual construction of the interdisciplinary collaboration model of team behavior that emanated from our study of the

Table 1.1.   Interdisciplinary Collaboration Model

	Stage One	*Stage Two*	*Stage Three*
Discipline Orientation	Dominant	Parallel	Integrative
Knowledge Engagement	Expert	Coordinated	Collaborative
Work Orientation	Individual	Group	Team
Leadership Orientation	Top-Down	Facilitative, inclusive	Web-like, servant

research team. While the dimensions of the model, in isolation, resemble findings from previous research by Tuckman (1965), Bolman and Deal (1997), Bensimon and Neumann (1993), and others, seeing the complementary and simultaneous development of the team across multiple dimensions presents a more complete and complex perspective. The stages are not time bound, but we believe they are developmental in nature. Each stage is briefly described below and discussed in more detail in subsequent chapters.

Stage One—Traditional (Dominant/Expert/Individual/ Top Down)

In Stage One, the group was preoccupied with the tasks of group formation, role and goal clarification, task allocation, and paradigm exploration. Members viewed project problems and intervention strategies through their own disciplinary lenses and behaved as though they alone had the answers. The group exchanged information but functioned and thought independent of each other. A primary focus of individuals was positioning themselves to have their disciplinary paradigm dominate. As a result, disciplinary clashes were frequent. Members were knowledge experts expecting to work individually on tasks. Leadership in Stage One was traditional (top down) and dealt with visioning, decision making and conflict resolution. This stage represented the traditional research/consultant approach to community interventions.

Stage Two—Transitional (Parallel/Coordinated/Group/Facilitative)

Stage Two was characterized by aspects of group norming, refining and coordinating work processes, leadership transition, and paradigm cohesion. It was an active, task-oriented period, and group members met more frequently. Competing paradigms existed in parallel; tasks were done independently and brought back to the group to be put together. Members remained committed to their disciplinary orientations, but also began to acknowledge that other members' paradigmatic contributions had merit in some situations. Trust, respect, and ownership grew in this stage. As they began internalizing the concepts and language of others, team members found the intellectual neutral space to move forward in their team development. Conflicts still occurred but members were better able to work through them and stay connected. This let the leadership model shift somewhat from traditional, more authoritarian leader behaviors to one where the leader's behaviors were more facilitative. Members began to address issues collectively and hold each other accountable rather than relying on the leader to handle all team maintenance and group dynamics.

Stage Three—Transformative (Integrative/Collaborative/Team/Web-like)

We cannot fully describe Stage Three because the research team we studied was not completely engaged in this stage at the time our data collection ended. So part of this stage is dependent on our conjecture of what the dimensions look like in more fully developed states. We hypothesize Stage Three as one of internal integration and collective cognition.

Individual members did not replace their paradigmatic lenses with new ones in Stage Three but rather used adaptive lenses reflecting the learning they did from and with other team members. They were now able to recognize contributions of once competing paradigms, so the need for intellectual dominance was gone. Communication was high in this stage and team members were motivated by the intellectual and cognitive learning taking place as much as they were by completing their original objectives. Shared values were internalized and acted to guide team behavior and cognitive growth. These values allowed for leadership to flow more freely through the team members based on the project needs. The team more appropriately handled crises and shared responsibility for their behavior, decision making, and product delivery. In a sense, in Stage Three, the team evolved into an interdisciplinary team where disciplinary boundaries disappear and new disciplinary perspectives, and new knowledge, could be created.

PROCEEDING WITH THE BOOK

We have organized this book in two main parts. The first describes in greater detail the interdisciplinary collaboration model as we saw it develop through our research team. We devote a chapter to each stage of the model, reviewing the different dimensions and showing the stories of team members as they lived these dimensions. We also develop the two themes of group process and paradigm exploration, which became useful organizing frames for us as we interacted with the team members on their interdisciplinary collaboration journey. In each chapter of the book's first part, we also describe for the reader those observations we had of the activities, issues, and learning components that characterized each stage. To some extent, these observations begin to place the findings from our research team into the relevant literature on group processes, team development, and leadership. We also share some understandings that seem more unique to our research team and the concept of interdisciplinary collaboration.

The second part of the book examines the data from our study through four analytic frames—structural, cultural, intellectual, and leadership—looking at interdisciplinary collaboration from both organizational and individual lenses. We conclude the text by moving a step back from our findings, and take time to think more broadly about interdisciplinary collaboration. We focus discussion on the larger constructs that emerged as important for the research team we studied, and that we believe have more general applicability. We also consider ways in which interdisciplinary collaboration as a form of faculty work acts as a vehicle for creating organizational change—for breaking out of the conventional academic box in which faculty often find themselves.

NOTE

1. A detailed description of the research design and methodology for this study are located in the Appendix.

CHAPTER 2

STAGE ONE

Tradition

Stage One of the interdisciplinary collaboration model represents the traditional research orientation commonly found in most research universities. It is a model that encourages and rewards individual accomplishments; one that follows the compartmentalized structure of the university; one that encourages the faculty to acquire a national reputation in their discipline. It is a model in which work is reviewed by disciplinary peers, and one in which career milestones such as rank and tenure are awarded on the basis of individual contributions to the department, university, and field.

The traditional research model represented in Stage One is a system that has worked successfully for more than a century and one to which it appears institutions other than research universities "drift" (Fairweather, 1996) and promote as they aspire to a particular kind of academic culture among their faculty. Historically, we have considered academic culture to be ingrained in the disciplinary structure of knowledge and knowledge acquisition (Clark, 1963, 1987). Students are trained, selected and rewarded for their success in the discipline and intellectual peers are often defined within a narrow academic culture. Each year, a new generation of scholars is trained and take their place among their disciplinary colleagues, to teach and conduct research and scholarship within a fairly nar-

Breaking Out of the Box: Interdisciplinary Collaboration and Faculty Work, 17–32
Copyright © 2004 by Information Age Publishing
17

Table 2.1.   Stage One—Interdisciplinary Collaboration Model

	Stage One	*Stage Two*	*Stage Three*
Discipline Orientation	**Dominant**	Parallel	Integrative
Knowledge Engagement	**Expert**	Coordinated	Collaborative
Work Orientation	**Individual**	Group	Team
Leadership Orientation	**Top-Down**	Facilitative, inclusive	Web-like, servant

rowly defined set of intellectual parameters. The realm of acceptable scholarly inquiry may be particularly strict for pre-tenure faculty whose ability to advance in the tenure system may be based in part on the extent of their potential for national recognition as a contributor to a particular concern, literature base, or area of scientific investigation. The traditional academic system perpetuates and regenerates itself based on the principle of individual accomplishment within the disciplinary structure of the university. Thus, it is not a surprise for faculty behavior to take an individualistic perspective in Stage One. Faculty are behaving in accordance to their professional indoctrination into academic ranks. They are enacting the role of expert in their field and are essentially embedded in the disciplinary trappings of their graduate training. This is the culture of academe.

Given the strength of academic culture and the longstanding traditions through which faculty are socialized into the profession, it follows that the developmental process of most faculty groups begins with Stage One behavior and beliefs, especially at research universities. However, our contention is that in reality, most groups start *and end* their tasks without developing beyond this stage. We find that most faculty groups exist without seeking or experiencing intellectual growth; without having to challenge the religiously held assumptions of their disciplinary training; without engaging beyond the safeguards of their academic identities as knowledge experts; and without moving beyond a definition of work that highly values individual contributions over collective functioning. And apparently, this is ok and often preferred.

Most university structures and reward systems foster and promote Stage One behavior, thereby tacitly (or perhaps intentionally) keeping faculty in this traditional mode. Fairweather (2002) notes that, even when faculty venture outside the narrow bands of traditionally accepted behaviors for team teaching experiences and coauthored publications, for example, review committees are often stymied about the process of evaluation. Committees then revert to weighing more heavily those aspects of productivity with which they have more objective confidence—solo-authored publications, single-class instructional models, and so forth. There is little or no expectation, encouragement, or reward to behave differently. Doing so often evinces a penalty at least in time spent circumventing or negotiating the organizational structure if not real cost, in terms of promotion and tenure. The traditional model of faculty productivity produces a recognizable and time-honored portfolio of academic work on which institutional and individual reputations are built and sustained. In some ways, it is efficient and as easily assessed as academic work might ever be. National rankings and academic classification systems reflect the values underlying this orientation, and as a result, it remains largely an intact postsecondary system in spite of conversations, research, and scholarly debate challenging it.

Yet, the traditional model tends to limit the potential for creativity beyond the discipline. In larger institutions, this may translate into the boundary of department structure. The model tends to recycle the same solutions to the same problems. Seldom are the issues permanently solved, and new knowledge is infrequently created or even used. New perspectives are rarely applied to old problems. New ways of thinking are rarely generated, or even expected; if they are, they may not be accepted readily. The disciplinary model, while highly successful in creating specialized knowledge, can also be limiting in creating new knowledge, at least as applied to addressing current and future complex societal problems.

There are a small but growing number of members in academe who believe that old problems require new solutions, and that addressing those problems through the current disciplinary configurations and departmental structures of the university will not generate needed insights and problem-solving strategies. These beliefs have led to more cross-disciplinary approaches to issues in hopes that multiple perspectives will ultimately lead to new and more creative solutions. It is this perspective that led to the research that fueled the development of our interdisciplinary collaboration model.

We acknowledge that any collection of faculty, including multidisciplinary work teams, will likely experience similar developmental processes to those we present, at least on some levels. Tuckman (1965) and other group dynamics authors have presented sufficient documentation of the ways in which groups evolve, even though they may not have studied faculty. Having said this, we also believe that the experiences of any interdisciplinary collaboration present some unique challenges, not the least of which are disciplinary clashes, faculty culture, departmental structure, and reward systems of the university. We explore the relationship of interdisciplinary collaboration and these organizational factors in later chapters of this book.

DIMENSIONS OF STAGE ONE

As part of analyzing the evolution of our research team, we looked at members through the four dimensions of the interdisciplinary collaboration model: disciplinary orientation, knowledge engagement, work orientation, and leadership orientation.

Discipline Orientation

In the first dimension of disciplinary orientation, faculty were committed to their disciplinary paradigm. Only one's personal disciplinary perspective was considered relevant and it was grounded in the disciplinary training each member received in graduate school or in their early faculty careers. Few faculty held more than one disciplinary perspective foremost in the way they conceptualized issues. They took in and processed information from one dominant discipline/orientation. One member observed, "Researchers at the university usually are very myopic when they think of research ... they only are interested in their own personal interests." In a group of faculty from various disciplines, members lobbied heavily to have the rest of the group adopt their academic worldview. Which disciplinary perspective was adopted by the group often was a function of who participated in the conversation and how vigorously one's perspective was argued over another. Members were not looking to apply multiple cognitive lenses but looking to have one perspective adopted— their own perspective, the one dominant perspective. Usually, individual members were unable to see the appropriateness or contributions of another disciplinary perspective, at least at first. Therefore, each member tried to argue the sanctity of their own paradigm or lens and have other group members adopt this perspective. Learning from others and reflecting on one's own knowledge biases was not a factor early in Stage One. It was seemingly easier or more appropriate faculty conduct to cajole others into accepting your view than it was to accept (or learn from) theirs. Debate was the forum that characterized Stage One.

Knowledge Engagement

In the knowledge engagement dimension of Stage One of the interdisciplinary collaboration model, members believed they were experts who viewed and interpreted the world most correctly through the use of their own disciplinary lens. Few members were comfortable or willing to have their expert role challenged, in part because to do so confronted disciplinary assumptions that were often so ingrained as not to be fully conscious. The group experience was not viewed as an opportunity to learn, but an opportunity to demonstrate and apply one's expertise in solving the presenting problem. As one person framed it, "[My role] was bringing in my skills and expertise to the project." After all, this was likely why faculty were asked to be members of a group in the first place (or at least they believed this was why), and that was the role they have historically been conditioned and asked to perform.

Work Orientation

Similar to the disciplinary orientation and knowledge engagement dimensions of the interdisciplinary collaboration model, and true to the research behavior of faculty, the work orientation of Stage One was from an individual perspective. In the beginning stages of work, the group was a collection of individuals. "It is not a team," says one member. "It isn't really a team.... Just working with that combination of people." As the group developed over many months, members began to define their roles in relation to others and perhaps even to the group as a collective. But in most cases, each member worked on a task individually. This was common even when more than one person was charged with a larger task. Orientation to academic work traditionally was to break the larger "chunk" into more discrete tasks that better represented the expertise of those involved, set off to accomplish the assignments individually, and then return in hopes that the pieces could be reconstructed into a whole.

Faculty used terms such as cooperate, coordinate, or collaborate to describe their experiences in working with other members of the group, often interchangeably. Yet, faculty worked by themselves to complete their part of a task, agreed on or designated earlier. In essence, they did their work and brought it to the group or other members. They completed a piece of the larger task. Their work was based on their disciplinary lens and expertise. There was no exposure to scrutiny by other members of the group. Because of the tendency to remain independent expert agents, we challenge the faculty's use of interchangeable terms to describe their work. Instead, we argue that there is a fundamental difference in the group and intellectual processes (and likely in the product) involved when people work in coordination, in cooperation, and in collaboration. At the heart of the interdisciplinary collaboration model is the decoupling of these terms and their meaning in collective work.

Leadership Orientation

Leadership orientation in Stage One followed a traditional bureaucratic model. The project administrator, who we often also refer to as the project leader, was the principal investigator for the funded research activity. She issued the original, broad invitation for participation, eventually put the working group together, called meetings, set agendas, had minutes recorded, controlled the budgets, and acted as the final decision maker. Although the inception of this particular partnership activity involved extensive discussions between the project administrator and another key member in thinking through the issues of a multidisciplinary team approach, members of the group attributed leadership to the project administrator only. Power and authority were top down. Members responded to the direction and vision of the project leader. In the words of the project administrator, her role was, "Administrative ... : developing the team, invitational role [for participation and for ending participation], keeping members focused on developing the program, putting infrastructure in place, identifying resources, steering, instigating the research component so we can be reflective about our work."

In the early stages of work, the project leader purposefully set aside time for paradigm exploration and reflection. Because the invitation to participate was intentionally multidisciplinary, the project leader expected differences to exist among members in how to proceed with work, what approaches to community development were most relevant to the issue at hand, and so forth. In fact, she hoped they would. So for her, initial meetings were anticipated to be spent identifying, articulating, and working through fundamental differences to arrive at more common ground for approaching the tasks at hand. As one member noted, "It was clear from the very first meeting that it was to be a partnership ... we had a very complicated project with a lot of different actors involved, so we'd have a variety of different viewpoints that would have to be merged together." And another remembered, "I guess early ground rules that established that this was going to be a working group ... and it was going to be an interdisciplinary group from various disciplines at [University]."

STAGE ONE OBSERVATIONS

Early phases of any group's development are quite active. This held true for Stage One of our research team's interdisciplinary collaboration development as well. When faculty from various academic units are brought together to accomplish a task, work on a project, or develop a policy, the group can initially be characterized as multidisciplinary, meaning a collection of faculty from different disciplinary perspectives who might exchange information but who function and think independent of each other. By definition, in the early stages of team formation, members view project problems and intervention strategies through their own disciplinary lenses and believe their perspective yields the best answer. One person in our research group presented his reason for participating, initially, as "to insure that the point of view of [my] discipline was included." During the initial period of group formation in Stage One, individuals in our research group were preoccupied with many beginning developmental tasks. They had to clearly articulate and clarify the goal of the group, work to define and specify each member's perceived role in the group, and determine the tasks that had to be completed to meet the goals of the group. This is true of most newly formed groups (Bolman & Deal, 1997; Ellis & Joslin, 1990: Harbert, Finnegan, & Tyler, 1997; Tuckman, 1965).

In the research team we studied, members viewed themselves as knowledge experts, involved to work individually on tasks. They responded to this situation in a traditional way. Two members noted, "[We each] basically just had one approach [to the job]," and "we were running our own agendas." The project administrator of the research group explained her perspective on the early work of the collective. She said, "[We used] a traditional response—respond to a request from a customer—a consultancy. We were brought in so we treated this as a similar event. I prepared the scope of work for the contract, laid out the tasks that needed to take place.... My anticipation was that team members would be assigned to deliver those tasks."

Group Process

Although the project administrator originally began the process of forming the group with the intent it should be multidisciplinary and lead to more innovative work processes and problem solutions, care and consideration still had to be given to the actual initial steps of bringing the group together. Stage One activities that include initial group formation are characterized as "forming and storming" (Tuckman, 1965) and our research group was no exception. "The project was particularly interesting because it brought into play an almost classical pattern of [disciplinary] conflict in the design," noted one member, commenting on the strong literature and research base supporting two of the primary disciplinary perspectives represented by members of the group. "[This] was in fact deliberately created by the project leader, who believed that both perspectives were needed in a successful intervention." However, on closer examination, there are reasons even a group more intentionally constructed falls prey to these traditional small group dynamics, as illustrated.

In our study, team members were curious of who other members were, what expertise they brought to the group, and why they chose to participate. The first invitational gathering, referred to as the "Call to Jesus" meeting, served as a way of presenting the project, potential scope of work, reasons for involvement, and other typical explanations given at the start of group activities. Introductions included the usual: name, departmental affiliation (disciplinary), and a short summary of recent research interests and experiences (definitions of expertise). The introductions began to define roles and disciplinary distinctions, almost by default.

The academic version of "name, rank and serial number" used in typical introductions seems to regularly serve as basis for identifying professional expertise and disciplinary orientation. Depending on the task, this may be appropriate and helpful. However, if the point is to encourage higher order thinking and collaboration, tacitly promoting traditional work roles, department affiliations, and disciplinary orientations inhibits new ways of working together and integrative thinking. More likely, it just reinforces the rigid disciplinary boundaries and identities held by each "expert" member of the team. Initially, members were not asked to introduce themselves through their interest in the project, for example. This might have provided a different communication base by highlighting over-arching commitments, goals, and common interests. In this way, members could see connecting points or the project administrator could more easily encourage discussion around the case problem regardless of institutional role.

These early meetings took on a particular aura as members situated themselves cautiously into the group. "These initial meetings were characterized by a distinct air of discomfort," noted one participant. He continued, "Staff from different entities in the university seemed to have differing agendas. There was conflict in the meetings. This conflict was most apparent in the nonverbal communication among staff. There even seemed to be a 'we know better than you' attitude among representatives from different departments."

As one member shared,

> The rules of the group have changed over time with the maturation of the group. At the beginning, it was a jockeying for positions, actually. People didn't know each other around the table. So who was in the group and why they are in the group and the identity of those people in the group needed to be developed, needed to be shared. And there needed to be an increased appreciation for the background and expertise that people would bring that would make them legitimate members of the group.

In subsequent meetings, conversations occurred around goals and tasks that further clarified individual roles. At this point, members began to get to know each other and anticipate how each might contribute their expertise and past experiences to achieving the goals of the team. As discussion progressed on goal and task clarification, the distinctive lines of disciplinary lenses began to emerge. One member characterized the early stages as, "From a group standpoint and from a project standpoint, we had at least four or five different points of view on what ought to happen in terms of basic theme and operation." Often, these perspectives were in conflict with each other, prompting some members to seek positions of power where their disciplinary lenses could become the dominant perspective employed by the group/team. This may not be articulated as "my discipline is more appropriate than yours;" sometimes, it was. As often happens in group dynamics, power took the form of, "In my experience" or "I have always found ...," thereby reinforcing levels of expertise and dominant ways of thinking.

Our Stage One observations reflect the myriad conversations, debates and conflicts experienced by the research team as they worked to adopt particular implementation strategies and training programs. Project work could be managed without reconciling paradigmatic differences because early tasks did not *require* a high degree of collaboration. The group operated as a very task-oriented, utilitarian team (Bensimon & Neumann, 1993). Individual members attended to their assigned, separate responsibilities and fed relevant information back to the group at meetings intended for information delivery and coordination (rather than dialogue and intellectual engagement of ideas). In the early weeks and months of Stage One, most group members perceived their role as being limited to specific tasks rather than feeling a sense of ownership of the whole, its processes, and its collective problem solving. Meetings were focused mainly on data sharing and articulating assignments rather than group processing, organizational learning, or forms of dialogue (Bennis, 1997; Senge, 1990). While this approach to project management allowed tasks to be accomplished, some members of the group were not satisfied with maintaining this way of working together. As one member described it, "People are not willing to be team players. Kind of this parallel, 'you do your thing, I'll do my thing.' I think that's got to go."

Conflict is inherent in any human resource organization (Morgan, 1999), including as a noted aspect of early group formation (Tuckman, 1965), and can have both positive and negative impact in its resolution. Throughout most of Stage One, conflict was less often resolved than it was suppressed. When discussion came to a head about defining the tasks necessary to work with the community, for example, it was evident that deep seeded ties to individual disciplines remained. The differences were sometimes temporarily explored, but typically, the group looked to the project administrator for decision making. The group had yet to adopt an integrated approach, even though project tasks were being completed. From an accountability perspective, therefore, the need to address the underlying tensions more fully was postponed in deference to staying on task with the funding cycle and project deliverables. This strategy was not without consequence, however. One member reflected, "[If the issue is not resolved], it resurfaces because there really hasn't been a meeting of the minds. People will listen in the group and then go on about doing whatever they were planning to do originally. I see it as a serious problem we still have to deal with. And from an interpersonal standpoint, it is a serious problem. We still have several undercurrents that need to be dealt with."

Paradigm Exploration

In groups purposefully formed to incorporate multiple disciplines, the role identity, goal clarification, and task formation that dominate early group activity can get particularly heated. This is true of most developing groups, hence the traditional allusion to "storming" (Tuckman, 1965). From another perspective, we might as easily relegate this period of positioning to personality differences. While there were personality adjustments to be made in our research group as well, our members tended to focus on the distinction or differences between disciplinary perspectives and approaches to addressing the presenting problems. These disciplinary and methodological clashes often pitted discipline against discipline; expert against expert; and defining differences against discovering commonalties. "It has been a consistent theme ... of differences and viewpoints on occasion resulting in ... a lot of creativity but also ... in some conflict," offered one member. Another described tensions in these early months saying, "I think another thing that created tensions was what I would call *prima dona-ism*." The project administrator intended for time to be spent exploring paradigmatic orientations of group members, so did not always reign in conflict. Clashes were common, especially as the group members with the two most frequently represented disciplinary orientations tried, unsuccessfully, to gain advantage over each other.

Disciplinary distinctions are a hallmark of research universities (Becher, 1989; Gumport, 1991) and many units have rich traditions of working with communities. The multidisciplinary approach was deliberate but risky, especially for a high-profile, community-based outreach project. In our research group, some members coming from an orientation that emphasized an economic approach to community building were in staunch conflict with those operating from a disciplinary perspective that emphasized building human capacity. Conflicts often arose and had to be handled by the project administrator in a nonthreatening way. "The main conflict that really emerged from our group is how to determine what was needed. We have [two disciplines] that never really worked together in the past," one member reflected. Historically, both approaches have been independently used in community-based projects and both have experienced failure in the long run. The project administrator knew this, and part of her hope was that, by working together, the strengths of both approaches might meld and yield a more productive community intervention. However, group members began the research project unwilling to acknowledge the limitations of their own approach or the potential contribution of the other(s). One member stated clearly a Stage One perspective on the value of her own disciplinary orientation: "At research universities, I think it is very important to have subject specialists involved.... I don't believe that just anybody can do what we are doing. That comes out of our discipline, our training in our research."

Because these were all members of the same research university and its specific organizational predilection towards research, the participants may well have expected the paradigm clashes they experienced during the period constituting Stage One of the project. Even so, comments of team members reiterated the tensions and divisiveness of this time together. There was one member who seemed able to see beyond tradition in the early months of the project. He articulated both his own willingness to see beyond his training and the potential pitfalls of bringing together disciplinary experts who were less interested in this approach when he said,

> I tend to be more eclectic in my way of doing things. I've been trained in different theoretical models, but I know theories and realities sometimes don't always mesh. And you have to pick a little bit from this discipline and a little bit from that discipline to make it work.... So with my way of thinking that wasn't a problem. But, it becomes a problem I think when you have purists in any particular discipline and they've been oriented to do certain things and even approaches [to the community]. Like social workers are trained to interact with community a certain way. Our urban affairs folks are trained to do it a different way. And then you may have disciplines that maybe don't even have a community orientation, but they have some expertise that we need to do what we need to do. The difficult thing is getting the experts to work together and agree on a common goal and say this is how we move forward.

Another team member explained the paradigm conflicts this way, "It has been ... consistent.... We had a very complicated project with a lot of different actors involved, so we had a variety of different viewpoints that we'd have to merge together. We would try to hammer out [our different points of view] until everyone was reasonably well satisfied." A fourth person observed, "[There were] different perspectives so clearly being articulated to a point where people weren't listening to each other. We were so tested, the tensions were so great, that civility broke down at times. There was a lot of yelling at times."

As is often the case, especially with funded research activities but also with other kinds of institutional group work, individuals are brought together, charges "delivered" to them, deadlines set, and the floodgates opened. Seldom is sufficient time allowed or planned for group formation to really occur, with all its sundry exploration, time consuming brainstorming, oft-heated discussions, and deep thought. More often, as a result of the inability to spend time on the fundamentals of group formation, faculty revert to traditional Stage One behavior—hear the charge, identify roles defined by rank and job function within the institution (and therefore, presumed areas of expertise), divide work accordingly, set up meetings for information reporting, and establish a deadline for project completion. Such was the dominant tendency of members of the research group, as well.

Recognizing this pattern of behavior, the project administrator described, in hindsight, part of what she would have done differently in the early stages of the project. She explained, "The other thing I would probably have done is to have regular meetings to develop this sense of the whole, and there's a variety of ways things should happen, so we could make more explicit what we think of the different frameworks. Some people would be able to, rather than after the fact, be able to anticipate that and to have managed that part of it better." In thinking about the early weeks of the project, one member's comments about her own participation paralleled those of the project administrator's general observations about the members: "I think the team did not have a clear understanding of what methodologies and expertise we could bring to the process."

We noticed the discontinuity common with developing groups when we asked members to talk about their early participation in the research team and the ways in which the project got established. Their comments mirrored those of the project administrator and also showed multiple, and sometimes conflicting interpretations of the early months of the effort. To illustrate these divergent views, several voices from group members are included. For example, many members agreed that more time spent at the beginning identifying project goals and parameters would have served them well. They shared, "[At the beginning, we needed to] pay more attention to defining what the roles in the project are, what the parameters of the project are, the goals of the project … a clear understanding of how each stakeholder involved in this project was going to participate, and that they couldn't be just a stakeholder/gatekeeper, that they had to be a stakeholder/contributor." "It's been a year and a half and we feel we have done much of nothing except work on process, preparing to do the work. And working on collaborative projects, I know that that's an important characteristic. At some point, you've got to say, 'You either are trusting or not trusting that this is an appropriate partnership and methodology.'"

> I'd like to spend more time in the beginning [of the group process] on rules, roles and relationships, and rules of operation … there is so much that has to be done and it had to happen so fast. I'm not sure it was truly possible … but I would like to start more from the beginning and let's spend much more time together going over exactly what are rules and how we are going to operate. This is truly what we want to do and how we are going to behave and that we would agree not to say things behind people's backs that we're not willing to say to their face. And that we would focus on describing things that would need to happen, rather than judging them. I'd like us to talk about goals and activities.

Critical project events often challenged the belief systems, commitment, and cohesion of the group during its early development, resulting in interpersonal and identity conflicts. At such times, group members often retreated into their disciplinary safe places, reverting to the role of expert and reneging on fragile relationships and alliances. The trust and respect developing among the group members was usually the first casualty of conflict. One person shared, "Trust is an issue with any group and it is an issue internally within [the team] because we had such different points of view. I mean you have to trust people and get to know one another, establish a relationship, and begin to have things be predictable." The project leader acted to maintain the trust and respect that was gradually growing as the team evolved.

Conflict was managed by the project administrator, when it was managed at all. The membership also relied on the project administrator to intervene and manage the conflict to an acceptable conclusion, like a mediator. Silent voices were invited to participate while louder voices were somewhat curtailed to allow more inclusive discussions. Especially early in Stage One, it was necessary for the project leader to have a strong presence in the group, while also managing all of the administrivia not apparent to the rest of the team. The members were still a group of individuals, and the project leader acted as the task master, visionary, final arbiter, and decision maker.

In many funded research, teaching and outreach projects, a difference often exists between the vision for the activity and the reality of time constraints. We have no reason to believe that the paradigm explorations and early group identity exploration of our research group were any more or less ambitious, divisive, or problematic than other cross-disciplinary activities, and perhaps any collective experience (Magolda, 2001). The time involved with this front end "forming" behavior of the group (Tuckman, 1965) was considerable and required strong facilitation skills by the project administrator. Fortunately, because she did not represent any of the disciplinary perspectives invited to participate in the work, she was able to stand apart from the clash of expert opinions to a certain extent. At the same time, her experience with outreach activity cast her in a different role of expert that, while typically serving in the best interests of expediting work of the group, sometimes injected other tensions into the group discussions. The additional responsibility of serving as project administrator, accountable to all constituents far more directly than any one else at this stage of the project, also instilled a unique sense of urgency after awhile to resolve conflict and move on.

As noted, rarely is it true that funded scholarly activity allows sufficient time for participants to adequately work through the group dynamics issues that surround new collectives. Often, there comes a point where someone (typically, the designated leader) corrals the members, becomes more centralized and top-down in the leadership and decision-making orientation, and work becomes quite task-oriented rather than process-oriented. The timing of such actions rarely coincides with the group's developmental needs, and therefore, prematurely draws closure to the interpersonal negotiations. Common ground, shared visions and understandings, the culture and ability for dialogue, and so forth, are often not well developed as a result.

This leads to at least two natural outgrowths. The first is a continued need for more traditional forms of leader-centered rather than shared leadership. The second is maintenance of Stage One behaviors. If the group has not really "normed" (Tuckman, 1965), then it remains caught in the earlier behavior of forming. Strong wills win out over logic and dialogue; dominant, expert thinking prevails. Work remains vested in traditional patterns of allocation around position. Meetings continue to be reporting venues where discussion is limited because opinions are not truly valued. Issues recycle because they were not really resolved. Disputes continue to need "outside" arbitration by the project leader. In examining many typical faculty scholarly projects, we see evidence of both these outgrowths. In analyzing the group formation cycle, it may well be that the first two stages of group development according to Tuckman (1965) do not actually get accomplished in faculty teams before it is time to move along in order to meet the stipulated deadlines of work, be they contract specific or cyclical in the academic year.

Transition

While faculty still displayed the expert, individual disciplinary dominance orientation for the most part early in the group project, conflict also tended to cause a gradual movement toward a more cooperative/coordinated approach characteristic of Stage Two of our model. Although the faculty were not ready to accept or fully incorporate the groundings of other team members, they remained committed to the community with which they were working.

Eventually, the tension from the paradigm clashes also caused the team members to seek and construct a less stressful atmosphere that allowed them to work on tasks together. Subconsciously, the team looked for ways to depersonalize the disciplinary debates. They sought an intellectual neutral space, a demilitarized zone, which allowed them to more safely pursue their tasks and move forward together. They began to talk in the third person, referencing the community more frequently in discussions. They asked each other, "What would the community want?" rather than approaching the decision making from the more political and self-serving stance of, "I think it would be best if." This allowed them to begin to discuss issues without first attacking the opposing disciplinary perspective. "It pulled us out of [any] one person's conceptual way of thinking or framework," offered a member.

This represented early steps of dialogue (Senge, 1990) to us rather than the debating or defending of personal views that characterized earlier meetings. Group members were beginning to listen, to let go of their disciplinary dogma, and to try to work more together than apart. It is not possible to precisely identify a moment when the member behavior shifted, although in the life of our research group the change did not happen until almost a year into their functioning. What was evident was that this entry into intellectual neutral space was the beginning of a transition into a new way of functioning, what we considered Stage Two behavior. Team members began to see the contributions of other disciplinary perspectives, even though acknowledgement of this was not always raised within the formal group setting. Their work became more coordinated and less fractured. They began to work more as a group and less as a set of independent individuals.

SUMMARY

Stage One represented a very active and sometimes volatile stage. Faculty followed the traditional expert research model found in most universities. They perceived themselves as disciplinary experts who had the answers the group sought. They worked independently, and brought the solution to the group. Tasks and problems brought to the meetings were viewed by each member through their disciplinary lenses. Disciplinary clashes caused tension in the group as members worked hard to convince others to adopt their disciplinary orientation, their problem definition, their methodology, and their solutions.

As transition through Stage One continued, group members evolved in many ways. In order for the disciplinary clashes to ease and the group to move on, members had to find an intellectual neutral space where they could begin to listen to other disciplinary perspectives, to see how other disciplinary perspectives complemented their own orientations, and resolve some holes in their own thinking. Rigid disciplinary assumptions could be suspended as dialogue replaced debate. Rather than trying to convince other group members to change or to adopt a different stance, members began to reflect on their own beliefs and learn from colleagues. Trust and respect grew through this process. Obtaining intellectual neutral space was a requisite to moving to Stage Two.

CHAPTER 3

STAGE TWO

Transition

Stage Two of the interdisciplinary collaboration model represents a significant shift in the way the team functions. The skirmishes between members for disciplinary dominance are less frequent. Team members have settled in to roles with clearer understanding of how the roles of the other team members fit together. Tasks are more clearly defined and understood. Team members begin to feel ownership for the process and outcomes. Trust and respect for the expertise and disciplinary perspectives of others have grown. Members are more open to listening to the discussion and looking for commonalties in approaches. Debate is less threatening and less confrontational.

THE DIMENSIONS OF STAGE TWO

We continued to study the evolution of our research team by looking through the four dimensions of the interdisciplinary collaboration model: disciplinary orientation, knowledge engagement, work orientation, and leadership orientation.

Breaking Out of the Box: Interdisciplinary Collaboration and Faculty Work, 33–47
Copyright © 2004 by Information Age Publishing
All rights of reproduction in any form reserved.

Table 3.1.   Stage Two—Interdisciplinary Collaboration Model

	Stage One	*Stage Two*	*Stage Three*
Discipline Orientation	Dominant	**Parallel**	Integrative
Knowledge Engagement	Expert	**Coordinated**	Collaborative
Work Orientation	Individual	**Group**	Team
Leadership Orientation	Top-Down	**Facilitative, inclusive**	Web-like, servant

Discipline Orientation

Disciplinary paradigms of team members exist parallel to each other in Stage Two. Group members remained committed to their respective disciplines, in part because the work of the group did not yet require or engender a paradigmatic change. Members remained loyal to their disciplinary orientations but were willing to accept the functional applications of other disciplines for completion of team tasks. Members used disciplinary expertise to carve out a niche on the project and identified ways in which their perspective could contribute to completing the tasks. In a very real sense, the disciplines co-existed and acted in parallel to each other.

Task assignments reinforced members' continued reliance on traditional disciplinary orientations. Typically, tasks were allocated by the project administrator primarily based on the members' expertise and experience, although the work of members often generated new task ideas. For example, the financial expert prepared the first draft of the budget while the technology expert developed a community demographic data set. Although such reliance on professional expertise may not have led quickly to integrated disciplinary perspectives, it ensured that required tasks were done and materials developed at least as points of departure. And of course, deliverables and project benchmarks are always a relevant consideration in any team's efforts. At the same time, for members, there was no obvious need to compromise their paradigmatic orientation and little evidence for the group to believe products would be better if compromise, or integration, was achieved. In Stage Two, instead of trying to position their orientation as the "right way," group members seemed to acknowledge that certain disciplinary approaches addressed issues more appropriately than others did. This allowed several disciplinary paradigms to coexist and often mitigated group conflict. One member described the transition in Stage Two as follows:

> At times, when you have parallel disciplines, you have philosophically different approaches and even though you can come together and maybe meet and say we are going to do this ... you still have the disciplines sort of distinguishing how they go about it. Or we can even agree on what to do [maybe, and] then it becomes a matter of approaching methodology and process. Even if we agree on that ... there may be agreement ... okay the majority wants to do this, but I still feel ... sometimes I can sense ... that some folks, because of different levels of experience feel that they bring different levels of knowledge to bear and they maybe just "know."

The group continued to make progress on goal attainment, which at this point meant discrete (as opposed to integrated or complex) task completion. Members remained largely committed to and embedded in their discipline and own ways of thinking.

Knowledge Engagement

The second dimension of the model, knowledge engagement, we characterized as coordinated in Stage Two. Tasks began to be viewed holistically by group members, as part of a larger project. A recognizable work plan for the project was developed. The efforts of the members were more coordinated. Members still applied their disciplinary expertise to their assigned tasks but the product was then brought back to the group for review, discussions, and modification. Full-fledged critique was not expected nor necessarily welcomed by other team members in the early phases of Stage Two, but comment and discussion were understood to be part of the emerging team's development. The group moved beyond using meetings only for reporting out, and instead, began to consider at least part of meetings to be discussion and "thinking time." More time was spent intellectually engaging with the subprojects on which others worked to offer thoughtful comment and constructive criticism, brainstorming next steps, and helping the project leader generate responses to outside constituents. One member characterized this new dimension of knowledge engagement this way: "I'm interested in getting better at the things I'm not very good at, you know and learning from people that have different points of view and different approaches that I don't understand."

Although tasks were still allocated most often based on professional expertise as noted, there was a distinction in the way expert knowledge was interpreted in Stage One and in Stage Two. The political posturing in

Stage One to force others to adopt one's disciplinary perspective as "right," hence "expert," shifted to an acceptance of the importance of different disciplinary explanations and strategies for addressing specific aspects of the problem. This could be interpreted as channeling the expert knowledge, allowing individuals to laud their expertise over defined areas of the project rather than letting one perspective drive the project, in all areas, from the beginning. Perhaps this was the case and a clever leadership ploy to buy time for the natural evolution of groups into more collective thought processes. Equally possible, channeling knowledge expertise was a way to retain commitment of group members because they continued to recognize their unique contributions to the project and as a result, were able to justify participation in their home departments. The channeling may also have just become a way of quelling arguments and paradigm clashes that waylaid the group during the first stage and at times, seemed to threaten progress on the group's overall deliverables.

Regardless, the coordination of knowledge in Stage Two was reflected by less paradigm competition. There was more latitude afforded by members to individual voices and a slowly increasing level of professional respect and acceptance. Discipline-specific knowledge was seen as *a* piece rather than *the* piece of the puzzle. The complexity of the technical assistance model of the project's funding contract continued to demand new and different areas of expertise to address emergent facets of the project than those originally present at the table. Members began to recognize and accept the value of contributions made by others to overall goal accomplishments even if they did not always fully agree with the choices made or styles used.

Work Orientation

During Stage Two, members also began to raise questions and express opinions outside their own disciplinary expertise. This seemed to represent several aspects of growth in both knowledge and work orientation, as the individuals started to work more as a group than was true in Stage One. Members started to listen to and engage each other in conversation. They became less defensive about their work and took in the feedback of other group members. They explored ideas with each other in ways that did not occur when the focus was internal and individual. Trust and respect among the membership grew. As one member commented, "Communication and trust [are effective ingredients of a team, and] I think that only comes about through understanding the hows and whys and what that each ... individual is going to be putting forth. And I guess communication only comes through lots and lots of contact [and conversation]."

Members began to feel ownership for the process and the project in its totality, rather than just feeling responsible for sub-parts of the project. There was a growing sense of the big picture, the gestalt. Members were no longer a mere collection of individuals. One person recalled, "[We began to talk about] which approaches seemed most salient, most useful, and what came out of that was an approach that was different than anything that was put on the table. We've changed the thinking of people. I've come to this thinking about parallel integrated development ... people doing their own part in a very parallel fashion."

We characterized this early evidence of collective ownership as group orientation to work. Yet, we also found it useful to think about this group orientation on a deeper level than simply a set of persons meeting regularly together who each made individual contributions to goal attainment and task accomplishment. The group was still dominantly utilitarian in the way it worked together (Bensimon & Neumann, 1993), bringing professional expertise to areas of work and feeding information back to the project administrator. The seemingly subtle shift to a more coordinated knowledge orientation also allowed for movement toward what Bensimon and Neumann (1993) called expressive and cognitive teams. Expressive teams are those that provide mutual support and counsel, to some degree, to each other and to the leader. Their behavior is more integrated than what occurs in utilitarian teams, and this way of functioning creates a sense of connectedness among group members for their joint work. Cognitive, or thinking teams, are a third kind of team described by Bensimon and Neumann and are those in which members feel collective ownership for the intellectual process and sense making (e.g., raising issues, synthesizing ideas, monitoring constituent values and team behaviors, visioning), as well as for task completion. In expressive teams, and more so in cognitive teams, disciplinary and institutional status layers, such as academic rank and past practice, lessen. Group members begin to assert themselves in discussions apart from their own designated tasks and areas of professional expertise. One member's reflection of this period was characterized as: "We have a structure around which allows differences to come out; people are comfortable resolving them."

Bensimon and Neumann (1993) described several thinking roles of cognitive teams we saw early evidence of as our research team transitioned through Stage Two. These roles included voices regularly conveying to the team how actions would be perceived by external constituents (interpreter); voices reminding the group of ethical responsibilities of the work in which they were engaged (emotional monitor); voices continuing to challenge tacit assumptions (analyst and critic); and voices synthesizing ideas for the group so that work could move forward (synthesizer). The voices rotated among group members, becoming disassociated from traditional organizational hierarchy or title. For example, the project administrator who convened the group meetings was no longer the only person looked to or who took responsibility for synthesizing an issue before the discussion proceeded. That more group members played multiple cognitive roles in the group suggests a higher level of collective development and the beginnings of a real team (Bensimon & Neumann, 1993). "We were looking to get more academic synergy," shared one participant, "to have a campus group that met and shared experiences from multidisciplinary points of view and have an interchange between [the various disciplines]."

Leadership Orientation

As the group transitioned from Stage One to Stage Two, roles and tasks became more clearly defined, and trust and respect for group members grew. Members also began to feel more ownership and to become more active in the group process. The leadership needs of the group transitioned, as well. Greenleaf (1995) noted that as a team develops, establishes its own culture, norms, and control mechanisms, it can be more internally motivated and self-directed. At these times, a more facilitative leadership approach can be effective. We found this leadership approach was appropriate for our research team during Stage Two. Overall, group members were more confident and comfortable in everyone's role, including their own, and felt a sense of direction and ownership for the group process.

As a result of team development, the project administrator could take a more facilitative and managerial role than the authoritarian approach necessary in Stage One when the group was seeking direction and identity. It was still necessary for the project administrator to set the agenda, although others were more willing to offer suggestions about it. She still convened the meetings, and performed the requisite budgetary and administrative functions of the group, as well. But it was not necessary to manage the individual tasks, assess progress, or construct decision-making scenarios where group tasks were concerned. As noted, members were more active in communicating, sharing and decision making, and assumed this level of interaction was what was necessary to move the project along.

Although many attempts to resolve conflict between members were tried by the group, especially in this stage of norm identification and solidification, the project administrator was still expected to manage interpersonal conflict and become the final arbiter. Similarly, crises initiated from external agents were perceived by the membership as the functional responsibility of the formal leader. In referencing some of these conflicts, one member suggested, "There was still a level of distrust of what the university might do with their relationship to the community", and felt the project administrator needed to resolve this situation. Members were willing to offer suggestions and to help the leader think through alternatives, but the final decision making and the "doing" were left to the project administrator. Thus, while the members of the group displayed more willingness to be self-directed and less reliance on the leader for tasks and planning functions of the group, the project leader was still expected to invoke traditional top-down leadership actions in the more bureaucratic areas of group function such as budget and conflict management.

It is interesting to note that, as the group transitioned through Stage Two, there was a leadership change to a member with a more facilitative and inclusive leadership style. The original project administrator removed herself from the daily operations of the group but maintained budgetary and final decision-making authority. When crises arose and threatened the group, the members looked to the project administrator to resolve the crisis because they had always seen her as a strong leader. However, the project administrator was not needed for task management and information sharing that accounted for the bulk of the group activities during this time. Clearly, the leadership needs of the group had changed and were appropriately accompanied by a change to a more facilitative leadership style. In describing his approach, the new leader (who we call the transition leader) expressed, "I think of myself as being responsible as an enabler in the project. By that, I mean being responsible for trying to see that the different points of view in the project are brought together and issues are identified and that they are resolved—to establish a structural process where other people can do their best work." We believe this facilitative style coincided with the growing confidence and ownership of the group members.

One aspect of leadership that carried over from late Stage One and that was a role both leaders played in the group was helping to develop common language. Perhaps more than other group members, the project administrator and the transition leader saw the importance of language to the overall group process and maturation. They consciously spent time facilitating conversations and were unwilling to abandon group discussions even with time pressures because of how they viewed the importance of this aspect of communication and culture. They believed that the strength of the team, its processes and products were closely tied to the development of a strong culture. And shared understandings and language, as much as academics might allow, were cornerstones of this cultural goal.

The centrality of this cultural component was made clear to both leaders whenever member transition occurred, and when individual members were "regressing" into disciplinary silos (Klein, 1990; Salter & Hearn, 1996). Although they worked to challenge members' thinking appropriately, the two leaders were not always successful in cultivating a strong group ethos and understanding among all members. The role of cultural leadership, including fostering shared language, is important in team development (Morgan, 1999) generally and certainly was important to developing this interdisciplinary collaboration effort. And by shared language, we do not mean just common verbiage but a common understanding of the meaning of the words. It was a particularly interesting challenge in an interdisciplinary collaboration among academics where, for such a long time, jargon defined identity of group members.

STAGE TWO OBSERVATIONS

As was true in Stage One, Stage Two was a very active period. In many ways, activities resembled those of the previous stage at first glance. Tasks continued to be generated and accomplished. Meetings continued on a regular basis and increased as work became more coordinated and specific tasks more complex. Members labored at understanding each other and respecting different orientations. The transition leader still played a recognizable and important role in overall group functioning. At the same time, many group behaviors and activities in Stage Two were unique and developmentally "advanced" from those in Stage One. Of particular note in studying an interdisciplinary team is the transition from the traditional group developmental processes of "storming" and "forming" to "norming" (Tuckman, 1965). In some respects, the phase of norming in group development is closely aligned with the ability to work in an interdisciplinary collaborative. Both require a common understanding, common language, shared values (at least to some extent), and a much closer intellectual connection than was necessary in the early stages of group work.

Group Process

During Stage Two, the group continued to refine its goals and the roles individual members would play in an on-going manner. Through meetings and discussions, members developed a better understanding of how their roles connected to each other and the ways in which each member could contribute. This should not imply that roles were staid—once and for all determined—nor were contributions set and unchanging. But unlike in Stage One, where posturing and politically intellectual positioning were the norm, Stage Two was characterized by a more mediated sense of the group. One member observed, "Meetings remained task oriented, but it became appropriate to have disagreements among staff without conflict." The members were in for the long haul. They understood there was little advantage to pigeon-holing each other into narrow work slots. One member reflected on his relationship to the group in Stage One and early phases of Stage Two this way: "The other tension for me was that I was representing all of [my discipline]. So I was sort of, you know, stuck out there as *the* person and I felt tokenized, I think, a little bit on a unit level, and used.... This is an important [tension]." During Stage Two of the team's development, when members started to listen more carefully to others' perspectives and to speak outside their disciplinary lenses, this member's feelings of disciplinary tokenism and expertise defined in narrow terms began to wane.

Members also came to believe that, as long as the process continued to unfold on behalf of the overall project goal, the project administrator was not going to eliminate tensions and conflicts by removing someone from the project. This began the shift of responsibility to group members themselves, and advanced the thought that members needed to figure out how to work together. "One of the things that I've been sensitive to, and I think I've been able to step away from then and objectify is that we're all changing our roles in the process," one member shared.

One way in which this evolution was visible was that communication in all forms increased during Stage Two, including between members outside of designated meeting times. E-mail, phone conversations, and spontaneous conversations were more common during this stage. These extra-meeting interactions were also focused productively on the group's work, rather than being used to undermine individual group members or heighten one's own perspectives and status within the group.

As indicated, the group was beginning to enact Bensimon and Neumann's (1993) cognitive teams. Members exhibited relationships with each other that suggested stronger commitment to the group and the group's collective efforts; they also reflected a higher level of team development. One member described the evolving group process in this way:

> The good thing about this team is that we did meet monthly. We had a debriefing session to say what happened ... what can we do differently, what do we need to do next, those kinds of things. And we listen to everyone. All the different disciplines, I think, helped because I might have felt like we

can do this differently, or we should have done that, and someone else might have said, "But that worked." … So I think that kind of team approach kind of helped…. And we can agree as we sit around a table … it didn't necessarily mean that we were right or that we made the right decision, but the process was to be inclusive and to agree before we moved ahead.

Paradigm Exploration

While not all of the membership fully bought into the processes of Stage Two, the majority of the group was recognizing the larger picture. Some even saw the value of the group having been intentionally constructed as multidisciplinary in nature. Subtle sanctioning behavior began to emerge as those who continued to act in the disciplinary dogma characteristic of Stage One felt the effects of the group's conscious brow beating. Norms were forming and those who were not in accord began to feel less connected and more distant from the central processes of the group.

In Stage Two, members were transitioning from paradigm clashes to a more civilized, "peaceful" coexistence. In a sense, the multiple paradigms represented by the members existed in parallel. One member shared, "Over time, I would say dominant was the beginning factor, when one disciplinary approach dominates the other. As a matter of process, I think it went to parallel. So what I see happening is … it's like a patchwork where you've got this and this and this. And they're all sort of put together, which looks probably different than it would at the beginning. So that's why I say parallel…. Disciplines were not melded together."

Because it was still uncommon for more than one group member to work on a task, the actual pieces of the project continued to be crafted in disciplinary isolation and often continued to be assigned based on professional expertise. Yet, because the norm was now to bring the product back to the group for feedback, and not just accountability, the individual pieces were becoming better-rounded and "intellectually available" to all group members. This process allowed members to recognize and acknowledge that certain approaches addressed some issues better than other approaches. They were slowly developing a common language and taking time to share more conceptual aspects of products so that others could see the reasoning behind particular decisions and/or discuss alternative scenarios and ways of accomplishing end goals. Members were more tolerant of the existence of parallel paradigms, which helped to mitigate conflicts among the team members based on discipline. Unfortunately, the tolerance for intellectual differences did less to help with the personality-based conflicts that continued to affect the team. Disciplinary specific knowledge was now seen as part of a larger intellectual puzzle. It was also viewed as something that could be shared with others, at least in part, rather than necessarily kept close to the vest as a way of maintaining professional status within the group.

One person commented on a specific confrontation between members with divergent perspectives that seemed to reflect this movement, albeit slow progress toward cooperative understandings and knowledge engagement.

> The subgroup included a variety of staff with different points of view. I decided not to give in on my view, but did not want to try to railroad it through the subgroup either. I approached the subgroup with a goal of making our different views visible and developing a set of principles and direction that blended our perspectives. We were able to agree on an approach that balanced our interests.... I believe that confrontation and resolution did a lot to bring us together in a common effort that merged our perspectives into a more unified whole.

The role of common language development as a reflection of an early shift toward Stage Three thinking was articulated by one member who was not a designated leader of the team. His comments showed the importance of common language to several aspects of the interdisciplinary team, a sense of belonging and ownership that were developing over time.

> Something happened about two months ago when it was actually starting to come together. And we started talking about the same things. That sort of adds to that level of trust. It was interesting because about a month ago, when we [went down to the community] I could have easily spoken for [another team member]. I probably could have, it wouldn't have been appropriate, but I could have done it if I absolutely had to. I could have spoken for [that team member], I could have spoken for [project administrator], and I could have spoken for [the transition leader]. I could have spoken for other people who were involved in the project. Because now we have kind of this common language, way of describing it that I think is interchangeable.

Later, he reflected further on the importance of sharing a common language to the potential effectiveness of this kind of faculty interaction. "[Our effectiveness is affected by] developing a common language. More of an appreciation and understanding of where we're coming from, how we can fit in the whole." This member's comments showed that having language that cut across disciplines not only was related to work but also to how members saw themselves connected to the team.

A late-comer to the team who struggled with membership issues throughout the period of time that we studied the group did not have quite the same shared understandings. She commented on the impact of not having quite integrated into the team by Stage Two when she said, "We have to remember that we weren't meeting with the rest of the team [initially], so we didn't know what they were doing and they didn't know what we were doing…. I think there's more of an understanding now … than what was at the onset. But I don't think there's a clear understanding yet of how each one of us fits into whatever the overall parameters of the project are." Another member who came into the project work later than others said, "Clearly, we're not integrated. I think our problem has been on multilevels, you know. We've been working in isolation from the rest of the team…. I don't think there was enough understanding about what our mandate was vis-à-vis other people." These divergent perspectives spoke to the different places members were in their own development along the interdisciplinary collaboration continua, and to the need for continued team maintenance by the leader(s). Because not everyone transitioned together in all respects, there was always a need to monitor the pulse of the group and to work at cultivating a strong intellectual and team culture.

Neutral Space

As stated earlier, the tension from the paradigm clashes that characterized Stage One interactions caused the team members to seek and construct a less stressful atmosphere that allowed them to work on tasks together. They found an intellectual neutral space, a demilitarized zone, which allowed them to safely pursue their tasks and move forward together. Establishing an intellectual neutral space was a mechanism that facilitated the tolerance for and fairly peaceful coexistence of parallel paradigms. "It pulled us out of one person's conceptual way of thinking or framework," offered a team member. This not only allowed the group to move into Stage Two, but also enabled the group to process and develop Stage Two behaviors.

The development of intellectual neutral space afforded the team members the opportunity to dialogue (Senge, 1990) and get past the disciplinary clashes characteristic of the earlier meetings and interactions. As members came to understand the basics and accepted the contributions of others' disciplinary perspectives, they spent more time listening and dialoging, rather than debating. An intellectual dialogue involving parallel paradigms was actually seen as a desirable activity by many group members. They tried to let go of their disciplinary dogma, and tried to work more together than apart. As noted earlier, universities are not organized to explore disciplinary differences, but the intellectual process of dialoging still seems inherent in the faculty psyche (Palmer, 1998). Once faculty got past debating the appropriateness of their disciplinary approaches and began dialoging about group tasks, they found the intellectual process as rewarding as completing assigned tasks. One member captured the essence of this stage in the developmental process when he reflected, "And I love working with the talent that we have involved in this project, and I like it that it is difficult. I like it. I like being stretched. And I like it that we have confrontations that make me uncomfortable. That's good for me, I think."

It was not possible to precisely identify a moment when the member behavior shifted, although in the life of our research group the change did not happen until almost a year into their functioning. What was clear was that this entry into intellectual neutral space was the beginning of a transition into a new way of functioning, that we called Stage Two behavior. The work of team members became more coordinated and less fractured. They began to work more as a group and less as a set of independent individuals. This was conveyed by one member who shared, "It was much easier to go with the ebb and flow of the project without constantly having to work around a fixated position, and the project is unfolding in a formative way that looks very different from expectations going in. And this, for me, is the fascinating part of the process—to see what gets created at the other end." Providing an intellectual neutral space suspended the disciplinary clashes, at least for blocks of time, and allowed for a safe environment to explore disciplinary differences. This was a critical step in facilitating the movement into and through Stage Two.

With faculty dialoging and problem solving, the potential for alternative perspectives and the creation of new knowledge was greatly enhanced. Fueled by the intellectual appeal of this process, group members began to put aside their disciplinary suppositions, the last barrier to integrative thinking and the creation of new knowledge systems. In thinking about the group's status in Stage Two, one member shared:

> The central ingredient is communication, but not just any communication, honest communication. They have to establish a trust relationship and having established a trust relationship, people have to trust enough to share their innermost fears, anxieties, angers, frustrations. We have to establish a structure for regularly communicating those issues, establishing feedback on how we are doing it. We have to go further in our souls about what our common vision is. And how to get there. We've gotten quite a bit there. I think we've still got further to go. We have to have a structure around which allows those differences to come out or a process where more people are comfortable resolving them, and closer integration between us…. We have to have a true belief that change can occur.

We heard the group's movement and development in this member's observations, and the depth with which he interpreted the learning taking place in this attempt at interdisciplinary work. Rather than simply dismissing the interpersonal issues inherent in group work, this member saw them as critical to faculty success. We certainly saw his comments reflecting a level of commitment to the group, to the project, and to learning and development that is not always found in more traditional divisions of labor or group work.

Because of the many ways in which the group was developing norms and becoming a cognitive team, issues of membership and team stability were important considerations in Stage Two. As one person described,

> I began to notice some of the tension easing in the group for three reasons. First, I began to sense a feeling of belonging to the group as my participation increased. Second, I began to sense a reduction in the tension and hostility between [the two major disciplines represented] in that they respected the work I had done.... Finally, I began to realize my own professional myopia in the project... I learned through trial and effort that a blunt approach can be too overbearing and can have a negative impact on getting a point across. Others began to lose their professional (and political) myopia in the project. I also began to notice a shift from individualized agendas to a more collective, collaborative, cohesive approach.... Pardon the metaphor, but it was as though once a state of equilibrium and "squeaky parts" of our mobile were ironed out, we became much more receptive to the shifting winds from the project itself, and, as a result, began to move more in tandem and in cycle with the pulse.

Although certainly this person's remarks initially reflected his own standing and feelings of connection with the group, his observations were repeated by others as they commented on their own experiences at this stage of the group's development. He also articulated changes in his perspective, as others did, from an individual agenda to collective thinking and purpose. Clearly, finding neutral space enabled the research team to move into Stage Two and begin to practice and internalize the behaviors of this stage. Neutral space allowed the team to listen and blend their disciplinary perspectives and see the project through a more holistic lens. The foundation for creating new knowledge was now in place.

SUMMARY

During the course of our study, we noticed shifts in the way group members behaved, in the way they thought, the way they completed their tasks, the way they worked with each other, and the way they were led. As they began to work on individual tasks, the dominance of members' disciplinary paradigms became less important to the overall task completion of the group and to the members, themselves. Evidence of this shift came as individual tasks were presented to the group and members began commenting and participating in assimilating the task into the larger project picture. While tasks were completed in parallel fashion, members began to see the holes in their individual perspectives. And they began to view their efforts in connection to the work of others in the group.

As the group developed trust and respect for each other, team members began to be more open to the opinions of others and to critique their own work. Members did more dialoging and less debating, coordinated and shared their tasks more openly, and began to see the group's work in a holistic manner. Leadership needs of the group were more facilitative and maintaining of the group's administrative components, and less directive. Members behaved as a group in decision making, task redefinition, and strategy development. Individual member behaviors were sanctioned by group norms more often than they were controlled by the project administrator.

Clearly, the group was evolving in their interdisciplinary thinking and the way in which they worked together. Their leadership needs significantly changed during Stage Two from bureaucratic directives to administrative maintenance. These are all prerequisites for movement into Stage Three.

CHAPTER 4

STAGE THREE

Transformation

Stage Three of the Interdisciplinary Collaboration Model represents a significant shift in the way the team thinks. Disciplinary distinctions are blurred as members now use adaptive lenses that recognize the contributions of various aspects of once competing paradigms. Team members have worked closely together enough that they understand the way their colleagues think and have, themselves, adjusted their own thinking. In a very real sense, members have integrated their disciplinary perspectives with those of their colleagues. "A patchwork" has been formed, as one member describes. Trust and respect among the group members have much more fully developed. Members are as motivated by the exchange and intellectual interplay with their colleagues as they are by accomplishing the goals of the group. The group has developed into a cognitive team (Bensimon & Neumann, 1993). This is the point in the team's development when new knowledge is a possible outcome of the team's integrative thinking and collaborative work.

THE DIMENSIONS OF STAGE THREE

We continued the study of our research team's evolution by again examining first, the four dimensions of the interdisciplinary collaboration model:

Breaking Out of the Box: Interdisciplinary Collaboration and Faculty Work, 49–58
Copyright © 2004 by Information Age Publishing

Table 4.1.   Stage Three—Interdisciplinary Collaboration Model

	Stage One	*Stage Two*	*Stage Three*
Discipline Orientation	Dominant	Parallel	**Integrative**
Knowledge Engagement	Expert	Coordinated	**Collaborative**
Work Orientation	Individual	Group	**Team**
Leadership Orientation	Top-Down	Facilitative, inclusive	**Web-like, servant**

disciplinary orientation, knowledge engagement, work orientation, and leadership orientation.

Discipline Orientation

Perhaps the most significant characteristic in Stage Three was the achievement of integrative thinking among the group members. Disciplinary paradigms moved from competing (Stage One) through coexisting (Stage Two) to integrated (Stage Three). Not only had disciplinary distinctions blurred, but members began to think in terms of adaptive or collective perspectives. They had not completely abandoned their disciplinary lenses, but they began to think qualitatively differently from their original disciplinary perspective. This thinking was a direct result of adapting to, and including other disciplinary perspectives. Members now recognized the significant contributions of various elements of once competing paradigms. Said one member, "It's a nice combination, an integrated combination." In this sense, the paradigm evolution was developmental. Members did not use their disciplines to compete for dominance but looked for ways in which they could complement each other as problems were further defined and resolutions created to address those problems. As a result, this was the stage where new knowledge creation could result from dialogue and the integrative perspectives that were spawned.

Our research team data did not show strong evidence that the team fully evolved to an integrative paradigmatic approach, although it was a clear goal for many. One person articulated his sense of the team's progress this way: "We are still skirting on the edges of [integrative]. We haven't completely moved into the integrative stage yet. [Sometimes, we are still] operating on one design and have an undercurrent of another, so I'd say an integrative approach is still my goal, but we are not there yet to complete it." When the project was going well and tasks were being completed, the team looked as if it was operating through an integrative lens. But when tested, team members often retreated to disciplinary "safe places" and it became more evident that the parallel paradigm was still in place. This is a common behavior noted by Klein (1990) when integrative thinking is still developing. One member's frustration with the periods of integrative "slippage" was characterized as, "I think to some degree that you can throw discipline sort of out the window and approach tabula rosa as they say, with a blank slate, you'll be more effective. Using what you've learned in terms of processes and how you get to the end results, your product, but not imposing that discipline, that other process."

There are a number of possible explanations for the lack of full integration, many of which are discussed later in the book. Time, goal and role clarification, the nature of the contractual relationship, the incentive and institutional support structures, and leadership style could all be factors that influenced the ways in which the team developed along the discipline orientation dimension. What is important to note is that, in spite of the fact that we do not believe the team had fully "arrived" in Stage Three of the interdisciplinary collaboration model, when they regressed or were overly challenged, they did not relapse nearly as far as they did earlier in their development. They also more quickly found their footing again and moved forward. As with other models in organizational or personal development literature, we see this shrinking scope of regression as evidence of solidification and maturing in a stage.

The person who assumed leader responsibilities for the team during Stage Two characterized the group at the end of our research study this way: "I think we made a tremendous amount of progress given the amount of learning that everybody had to have occur. So in the standpoint of the amount of time since the project began, I think it is extraordinary. But we are not there yet. There are still elements of dominance in parallel play, and a lot of growth in these to take place to know they are truly integrated."

Knowledge Engagement

In Stage Three, members had evolved from coordinating their tasks and sharing information with the group to a level of true collaboration. They applied the multiple yet integrated disciplinary perspectives to address the tasks at hand. Communication, both formal and informal, increased as ideas were exchanged and recreated. These intellectual and cognitive changes were the glue that held team members together as much as task accomplishment. They sensed something exciting and new was happening within the group. One member shared, "We're very excited about the project. I think it holds a lot of potential for integrating different perspectives ... we've got a unique situation here."

Members actively listened to each other, taught each other, and learned from each other. They had really evolved in their relationships to and with each other. Each member had a voice. As one person saw it,

> I don't know how much of it involved predominately trying to do it as an integrative approach, but in a sense it was evolutionary. We started out as one approach being done and then for a while, we engaged in parallel play. We had a subgroup designed to bring the different points of view together. We evolved in our group process from a dominate point of view to parallel to predominately consensus, although we still have elements of all three at one time or another coming up.

In this study, we found many participants who originally came to the project with definitions of collaboration much more reminiscent of Austin and Baldwin's (1991) cooperation; some did not move far from this vantage point. For example, one member firmly stated her commitment to the intent of this interdisciplinary collaboration at the same time that she articulated the paradox we so often find when faculty begin joint work efforts. She shared, "We are dedicated to collaborative projects ... we saw this chance of utilizing our training and our professional tools in a group project ... [my colleague and I] saw this as a real opportunity to take this and run with it."

Certainly, faculty always bring their training and professional expertise to any work effort. And we would not suggest they do otherwise. But we also hear in the words of this participant the challenges of moving out of Stage One thinking when working together on a project, through the transitions of the Interdisciplinary Collaboration continuum from cooperation to collaboration. This team member spoke of valuing the philosophy of collaboration, at least in the vernacular. In implementation, however, it meant taking the piece appropriate to her disciplinary training and "running with it," not working with others to determine collaborative ways of moving forward. It did not represent a value-added, generative approach to work or an expectation of cognitive growth on her part. This person struggled throughout the project period with role clarity, group goal identification, and feelings of membership. She was often also frustrated by the process orientation of the team, in deference to a more traditional approach to faculty work that emphasized product.

Work Orientation

The group had become a team in the way they worked together, especially when compared to their connections in Stage One. It was no longer simply a structure organized to achieve predetermined ends through prescribed roles (Bensimon & Neumann, 1993). Perhaps more important to the intellectual nature of interdisciplinary collaboration as we have defined it, the group had become a cognitive team as defined by Bensimon and Neumann with shared values, language and vision. Communication among members, both formal and informal, increased as ideas were exchanged and recreated. Trust and respect among team members was high as shared values were internalized. One member offered, "One of the things that reinforced [development of trust and respect among group members] was the fact that we maintained ongoing contact.... That helped us communicate differences in feedback mechanisms where we had a way of identifying where things were going on and making adjustments. We spent time together ... had a chance to establish a personal relationship."

Crises no longer threatened the group in significant ways but were seen as opportunities for further growth and exploration. Members shared responsibility for team activities, leadership, and decision making. They recognized there was something unique about the experience they were having together and were focused on the well-being of the team as well as its goals.

Leadership Orientation

The leadership needs of the team greatly changed since it was originally brought together. Active listening, reflection, and continuous learning were cornerstones of Stage Three. The team was highly adaptive to creating solutions and open to the free uninhabited debate of issues. Shared values were internalized, not merely intellectualized, and guided the development of the team's cognitive lenses. These values supplanted the need for authoritarian leadership, as leadership could now flow more freely through the team members based on the project needs. Members started to find ways to generate more internal (to the team) leadership and leadership opportunities.

In Stage Three, team members felt responsibility and ownership of the process and outcomes. One member might still be identified as primarily responsible for the group's administrative needs (budget, contracts, meeting minutes, etc.) but the group now was setting the agenda, reviewing the work, and developing future tasks and direction. Because of her full-time job at the university, the project administrator had to manage the bureau-cratic aspects of the team functions, especially since the team remained connected to and part of a larger university organization. Yet, the project administrator also became in other respects more of an equal partner, nurturer, and group maintenance person. Members did not look to either the project administrator or transition leader for decision making, though would trust either to make decisions on behalf of the team if time was a factor. "[Decisions are made] predominately by consensus," noted one member. "We continue to have [an issue] as a subject until everybody is at least, if not completely satisfied, willing to live with the decision." This represented a significant change from the early days of Stage One, when members vied for dominance in decision making and discussions. In this way, the project administrator and transition leader were able to focus on facilitating team processes, and could take a more servant-like approach to the leader role. Another member shared,

> We have to redefine the nature of leadership ... and by that I mean we need to evolve from a power-based model into an enabling model. We need to evolve from control and management into empowerment, and we need to move from ... a linear, "we do this and we do that, and then we do that," bulwark kind of model into a mobile where you have an evolving set of constantly changing relationships where you understand and view it in its entirety. We need to move more effectively from power-based relationships into reciprocal relationships.

Crises did not threaten the group and reopen old wounds but provided opportunities for the team to further develop their collective cognition (Bensimon & Neumann, 1993; Kuhnert & Lewis, 1989). Members shared responsibility for their actions and collective decisions. All members had grown to more genuinely trust and respect each other in the altruistic motivation and advancement of the team.

STAGE THREE OBSERVATIONS

Members were really still becoming fully engaged in Stage Three behaviors when we finished our data collection. So our observations of this stage are somewhat fewer than those we had of earlier stages represented in our interdisciplinary collaboration model.

Group Process

In Stage Three, tasks continued to evolve and were redefined as the team's cognitive perspectives continued to adapt. In addition to staying the course of the contract itself, the synergy of the team took it in different directions when generating new elements of the overall project and ways to accomplish emerging needs of the community. Team members were reflective of task completion and new problems that emerged, illustrated by these comments:

> I think as a group we made a significant developmental step. At least if we [don't] resolve the issue completely, at least we had the right issues on the table, but people could look at them over time. Those are things that are extraordinarily complicated for anyone to deal with. I mean it is a process of evolving…. In the earlier stages we were getting complete answers to the wrong questions. And then [neutral space] when we started on that, we were at least getting partial answers to the right questions. So we identified the major themes we were going to have to struggle with over the next year at this point.

Significant challenges were seen as opportunities rather than threats or annoying distractions. In many ways, the challenges were similar to those experienced in earlier stages, both within the group and outside of it, although sometimes of a deeper magnitude. What had changed by Stage Three was the attitude toward these challenges and ways in which team members saw their roles in creating and addressing them. All members shared responsibility for tasks, as the disciplinary expert form of consulting that existed in Stage One was replaced by a collaborative team. Issues across the areas of work and interpersonal relations of the team members were raised and decisions were made within the totality. The team functioned collectively.

Paradigm Exploration

Team members continued paradigm exploration. It may be that a new paradigm was in the initial stages of creation, as some authors suggest is the "true" measure of interdisciplinarity (Klein, 1990; Salter & Hearn, 1996), but we did not see this come to fruition. Nor we do we agree that new paradigms, or disciplines, are the necessary outcomes of interdisciplinary collaboration. At the point at which our data collection ended, we found it unlikely that individual members of the team would completely abandon their own disciplinary paradigms. Given the traditions of academic work and research, we are not sure that it is even reasonable or appropriate for faculty to leave their intellectual roots entirely, even if it was possible to do so. Nevertheless, team members' disciplinary perspectives evolved and were distinctively different from those they held in the initial stage of the project. As one person noted, "I believe we started as a group of highly qualified individual experts and are evolving into a team of people trying to blend their abilities."

In Stage Three, members now looked to complement others' disciplinary perspectives, and through intellectual discourse, adapt their own disciplinary lenses. In reflecting on the team's process, one member described the evolution of thought and engagement in which he had been involved as, "Across-disciplinary work, where you take different expertise and points of view and background, and try to integrate it." This represented a qualitatively different way of thinking than the members had when they attended the initial meeting about the project. For most, challenge to their way of thinking was far less a reason for initially participating than was the opportunity to exercise their disciplinary expertise and prowess in addressing the project's problems. For most, the 18-month interaction led them on a developmental journey across many dimensions of their professional lives they did not expect. And for most, one of the critical aspects of this journey was the realization of being in a new intellectual place—one that integrated the disciplinary orientations of others with their own.

We noted throughout the study period that as the team evolved, each member adapted their disciplinary perspectives at different rates. From a developmental perspective, this was not surprising. Some members were more integrative in their perspectives than others, but most had internalized new cognitive perspectives by Stage Three. Those perspectives were now distinctly different from the original perspective held when they joined the project. Team cognition represented a level of thinking that applied the multiple perspectives of the team members. Members thought collectively. From the perspective of team members, this evolution represented fundamental change, as noted by one who said,

> I see a massive accomplishment (for the time spent) really. We really only have been working on this for a year and one-half. Given the task at hand, I think that [group growth is] extraordinary because we are dealing with actual fundamental values and beliefs of all of us that have had to change, myself included. We're dealing with a complex multi-level system change ... that is, psychological levels, sociological levels, interpersonal levels, personality issues, economic issues, historical issues. It's like an onion with a thousand layers.

Another shared, "So we're all on this learning curve. And I like to think of it in terms of a mobile. I keep going back to that. When one shifts, the other shifts, the other shifts. So that's really what the whole process is about. It's about shifting. And coming to different states of equilibrium."

We do not want to imply that members regularly agreed, that the team acted without the typical group dynamics, and that the need for on-going team maintenance had evaporated. As one person noted,

> Like any group, most people in the group seem to be able to express ideas, some better than others. There are particular people who are willing and able to say, "this is wrong and I disagree." And to try to find a way to talk.... Like all groups, there are also other people who are not good at speaking their mind and who tend to speak their mind only outside of the group process, which makes it hard to do. And when that happens, I still see it as a serious issue and partly due to personalities and style, and by serious, I mean it comes out. If it isn't dealt with openly in the group, it comes out as manipulation.

What was different in Stage Three from earlier stages was the level of consciousness held by all members of how group dynamics were fundamentally important to team functioning, and members' greater willingness to assume responsibility for cultivating positive relationships. The same kind of conscious awareness was also present around issues of member voice, knowledge engagement, and leadership.

Theorists clearly suggest that organizational development is a slow process. Those who write of collaborative work and (real) team development argue that these processes are not only slow to evolve, but that they require high levels of maintenance, particular leadership styles, and certain environmental/organizational circumstances throughout the developmental processes (Bensimon & Neumann, 1993; Klein, 1990; Lattuca, 2002a; Salter & Hearn, 1996). This was certainly true for the research team we studied.

SUMMARY

It is difficult to flush out Stage Three in great detail because it was not represented fully in the data from our research team. Even so, in terms of our interdisciplinary collaboration model, we posit that Stage Three would be characterized by the internally integrated development of group cognition. Members moved in their disciplinary orientations from competing in Stage One through coexisting in Stage Two to at least complimentary if not integrated in Stage Three. They replaced debate in Stage One with dialogue in Stage Three.

Individual members did not replace the lenses of their paradigm with new ones but saw through adaptive lenses that recognized and incorporated the contributions of various aspects of once competing paradigms. They looked for ways in which other perspectives enhanced their own, rather than focusing only on the dissonant aspects of others' intellectual orientations. While the disciplinary paradigm previously held was modified in some way, sometimes in a truly transformative way, the fundamental core of the paradigm still remained intact for most. Yet, it was impossible for members to think as they once did; they experienced learning from each other and this learning was being internalized not just intellectualized. As a result, members saw the world differently and responded to each other and their collaboration efforts differently.

Because team members worked more closely together and collectively owned the team's outcomes, successes, and interpersonal maintenance functions more directly, leadership needs also changed in Stage Three. Leader behavior transitioned from a need for directive, authoritative actions enacted by a single designated person to more servant-like behaviors that supported the work of the team. Although there still was a transition leader identified for the team, leadership responsibilities such as agenda setting, synthesizing work, behavior monitoring, and socializing of new members were shared among the team.

Total internalization of the ideals of the interdisciplinary collaboration model had not been achieved at the point we ended our data collection. As we noted, and as team members also commented, it takes a great amount of time and effort to internalize and enact a paradigm shift such as the one we are purporting. There were also institutional, cultural, intellectual and leadership aspects that inhibited a "swift" or complete transition through the stages of our interdisciplinary collaboration model. Even after 18 months, the full shift from the traditional faculty behavior and approach to collective work to interdisciplinary collaboration had not completely occurred. At the same time, the evidence was clear that the team was continuing its development and that integrative thinking and problem solving existed for many members of the team. Perhaps of most importance to our study, those who remained with the project believed firmly in the interdisciplinary collaboration approach they were engaged in, the potential for creative (and effective) outcomes, and the intellectual capacity building that resulted from it. In support of this conclusion, one member reflected on the evolution this way: "We need to be engaged ... and use the interaction ... as a way of collaborating in both the discovery, in the integration, synthesis, application, and transmission of knowledge."

CHAPTER 5

MAKING SENSE OF INTERDISCIPLINARY COLLABORATION

Having described in some detail the interdisciplinary collaboration model and its stages, we want to move now to making greater sense of our findings and how they might apply to postsecondary education. In the remainder of the text, we think carefully about the implications of the interdisciplinary collaboration model in practice. Through studying our research team, reviewing the literature, and reflecting on our own decades of experience in higher education organizations, we see several spheres of influence on the particular form of faculty work presented in the early chapters of this book. We also see several frames for thinking about the impact of interdisciplinary collaboration and ways in which our present postsecondary systems need to change to better accommodate it. Although we do not advocate abandoning traditional, disciplinary-based faculty work and the structures that support it, we have come to believe in the merits of interdisciplinary collaboration. We also see significant impediments to its practice characterizing higher education today that need to be highlighted.

Our discussion proceeds by examining four spheres or areas of influence that can inhibit and/or support interdisciplinary collaboration: structure, culture, intellectual, and leadership. The last 3 decades of research on faculty work have shown myriad forces that shape faculty roles and

Breaking Out of the Box: Interdisciplinary Collaboration and Faculty Work, 59–62

academic work. In many ways, most of these forces were likely present for the research team we studied. Influences such as the labor market, institutional mission, compensation and contract construction, academic rank, departmental structures, external funding sources and demands are just some of the factors that have been shown to affect the choices made by faculty about how to spend their time and construct their work lives. To tie the experiences of our research team and the construct of interdisciplinary collaboration to each of these variables would be illogical and impractical to those interested in this form of work. Instead, we have chosen to look at these individual forces through frames that provide more complex and connected views of faculty work and its contexts.

There were many frameworks for looking at these data, each of which would have produced different understandings. We used frames that represent our own disciplinary orientations and that seemed to effectively capture an understanding of those factors that most shaped the decisions of those in our research team. Of course, other researchers could make alternate choices and might even organize our discussions differently within the lenses we chose. Regardless, in the next four chapters of the book, we have made distinct many aspects of faculty work and academic life that are intertwined in reality, and that define each other. So it is necessary to visit several issues from multiple perspectives in order to make sense of them in a deeper and more meaningful way.

First, we examine the structural components of higher education organizations that influence, and often inhibit, the practice of interdisciplinary collaboration. Many structural boundaries need to be crossed in order to successfully accomplish interdisciplinary collaboration without overly penalizing faculty for their participation. We focus on departments because these are organizational structures that most closely manage faculty life and where several of the key structural boundaries for faculty are located. (We recognize that institutional contexts affect the extent to which this is true, but since our research team was located at a research university, our analysis largely fits within that sector.) We examine alignment of bureaucratic processes and procedures at the department and institutional levels. We also take into account those structural elements of the faculty evaluation and promotion/tenure cycles because of the ways in which they affect faculty work. One of the more unique aspects of our study proved to be the importance of organizational neutral space. We consider the implications of having or creating alternative organizational structures specifically to support interdisciplinary collaboration.

Next, we look at the ways in which culture affects the practice of interdisciplinary collaboration. There are many different levels of culture applicable to an examination of faculty work and ways of conceptualizing the role of culture—discipline, department, institutional, and professional constitute just one scheme. Given our topic, we chose to emphasize the disciplinary culture and its influence on faculty work. At the same time, we acknowledge the extent to which cultural influences and understandings overlap each other, and simultaneously influence faculty beliefs, attitudes, and work. Considering interdisciplinary collaboration from a cultural perspective suggests the need to find some important cultural levers that could be influenced to create change or to support these alternate forms of academic work. We examine the role of graduate education and the socialization of prospective (and early career) faculty into traditional forms of knowledge engagement and disciplinary orientations, and the importance of rethinking graduate preparation to expand opportunities for interdisciplinary collaboration.

We also reconsider two areas discussed in the structural chapter: reward structures and matrix organizations. Although the reward structure for faculty has a structural component, it is also a kind of cultural artifact worth considering in terms of the ways in which it influences faculty decisions. Similarly, matrix organizations and other flexible work configurations are certainly appropriately viewed through structural frames. Yet, there are cultural considerations associated with these organizational forms that should be taken into account.

Perhaps one of the frames that emerged later in our writing and most surprised us for thinking about interdisciplinary collaboration was the intellectual and cognitive perspective. This seems an obvious oversight to us, now, but for a long time, we did not make conscious the extent to which we were interpreting the experiences of the research team as learning experiences. We were two researchers originally charged with studying team development and whose knowledge orientations are routed in different disciplinary definitions of organization. As a result, it took awhile for us to see this particular aspect of our data, or at least to recognize it fully as learning. Taking on the lens of cognition and intellectual development enhanced our understandings of the team experiences and led us to different ways of conceptualizing the leadership dimension of our model, as well. We look at the ways in which interdisciplinary collaboration becomes a form of learning for individual faculty and the team, itself. Aspects of this include dialogue and the development of common language. Unique to our study was also the clear evidence of what we called, "intellectual neutral space"—that moratorium or demilitarized zone that provided faculty an opportunity to transition between Stage One and Stage Two of our model. The importance of this intellectual concept was striking to us.

We then move to an exploration of part of our original charge—the role of leadership in interdisciplinary collaboration. How leaders facilitate this kind of faculty work, beyond the adage of "herding cats," was a mystery going into the project and, while not reduced to a set of generic steps, is more clear to us now. The question of whether or not a single leader can facilitate faculty throughout an interdisciplinary collaboration led us to look closely at the personal evolution of leaders in such a process. Does the leader have to move through a similar series of transitions as the team members? Does she also need to move from expert to integrative thinker? Does he also have to reflect, challenge biases, learn from others, and incorporate different disciplinary orientations into practice in order to effectively facilitate those transitions in team members? We include in our discussion several leadership challenges that surfaced including institutional challenges, team and cultural leadership, and membership issues that required leader attention. Although leadership research is replete with models, steps, and strategy lists, the "what" of leadership is often absent in the discussion. Not only do we have a specific "what" in mind—interdisciplinary collaboration—we recognize that the team process we studied is really a learning process. So in many ways, we studied the leadership of learning, including the learning of the leader.

Finally, we began with the intent of providing some cumulative thoughts about the utility of interdisciplinary collaboration, and lessons learned that others might use. Our final chapter offers initial thoughts about "so what" and "who cares." We consider the concept of neutrality and its importance in the development of interdisciplinary collaboration. We explore what would be required to expand the values of academic work to include interdisciplinary collaboration and the nature of organizational change that accompanies that expansion. And finally, we consider the leadership of learning. We lay out some thoughts about the orientation to leadership required to facilitate members through the transition toward interdisciplinary collaboration.

CHAPTER 6

INTERDISCIPLINARY COLLABORATION AND SPANNING BUREAUCRATIC STRUCTURES

For over a century, universities have been organized by a growing sophistication and specialization in the knowledge base. Professional schools, colleges, and departments have become the traditional means of organizing faculty and delivering courses in the modern university (Duryea, 1973; Mintzberg, 1979). The pressure to conduct research and publish has encouraged faculties to further specialize their expertise. As the knowledge base continues to narrow, and specialization draws faculty into a more focused quest to create new knowledge, the structure of the modern university continues to evolve into discrete little fiefdoms. Duryea noted that universities are a base from which faculty pursue their primary concern with research activities and the expansion of knowledge. He observed that specialization has produced a tendency toward fragmentation of the academic organization. As the press for research dollars and publications heightens in the modern university, faculties have become more fragmented and departmentalized today than they were even a decade ago.

While specialization and departmentalization of faculty has served society well, it has also acted to isolate faculty from each other (Clark,

Breaking Out of the Box: Interdisciplinary Collaboration and Faculty Work, 63–78

1963; Tierney, 1989). Faculties have become physically isolated from each other as campuses have grown in size. At research universities and many larger state institutions, most colleges and schools are housed separately in their own building or complex. Sometimes, they are even distanced by larger geographic expanses, as institutions have grown into conglomerates of "campuses" and "centers" often physically located off the main site. Departments are further separated by floors and walls as each unit tries to build its own niche for conducting research. The office or lab has become an inner sanctum where faculty can go about their own work while insulating themselves from the business of the university. These physical barriers are unintentional, perhaps, but act to separate and isolate faculty from each other, nevertheless. In many instances, faculty feel closer to their disciplinary colleagues across the country than they feel to their peers in another department across the hall. Ironically, technology, particularly email, has minimized the distance of miles and countries, but seems not to have shrunk the steps between offices or across campus.

Exchanges among faculty housed in different departments are often cordial, collegial, and almost superficial at times. Conversations revolve around the weather, current events, students, or issues in the work environment. Rarely do these conversations reach the level of crossing intellectual boundaries to discuss a common research issue, or seek intellectual integration of disciplinary concepts. Yet, we read often that faculty want this richer, more connected kind of exchange throughout their careers, and that in certain stages, including pretenure, the isolation they experience without deeper intellectual engagement is palpable (Austin, 2002; Boice, 1992; Menges & Associates, 1999; Rice, 1998; Rice, Sorcinelli, & Austin, 2000; Tierney & Bensimon, 1996).

It is this organizational context that acts as a barrier to interdisciplinary collaboration, among other aspects of faculty work and life. Faculty will seldom reach across the aisle to a colleague in a different discipline to engage in research efforts. Such efforts are not often encouraged, are difficult to support, rarely rewarded, and seldom seen as beneficial toward individual promotion. Individual research and disciplinary contributions (versus collaborative and interdisciplinary) are better understood by one's disciplinary peers and much more richly rewarded. Faculty who desire to participate in interdisciplinary collaboration efforts must do so on their own time, often at the expense of their other duties and responsibilities, and at the risk of their own careers. At least this is the strongly held belief. The careers of untenured junior faculty are particularly at risk if they participate in interdisciplinary and collaborative activities (Tierney & Bensimon, 1996). On occasions when interdisciplinary collaboration efforts have been encouraged by administrative initiatives, they have been short term, sparsely funded (or specifically funded, as in recent National Science Foundation funding mandates), and time consuming.

It has become apparent in recent years, and certainly to us in this study, that the organizational structure of the university, specifically the department, which has enhanced disciplinary specialization and the creation of knowledge, inadvertently discourages interdisciplinary collaboration (see Colbeck, 1998; Fairweather, 2002; and others for additional discussion). A number of institutional barriers to interdisciplinary collaboration efforts arise because of the disciplinary structures and departmental fragmentation present in most universities. In our study, we identified a number of institutional barriers that tended to discourage, if not inhibit, interdisciplinary collaboration efforts. Those barriers include the departmental structure, reward structures, budgetary procedures, and lack of organizational neutral space to house interdisciplinary collaboration efforts. We discuss these barriers in this chapter and make some recommendations as to how universities might realign themselves to encourage and support interdisciplinary collaboration efforts in the future.

DEPARTMENTAL STRUCTURE AND
FACULTY ROLE EXPECTATIONS

Organized around curriculum and epistemological concerns, the department has become an entity unto itself. Even as early as 1970, academic observers like Duryea (1973) noted that departments were potent forces for enhancing the university's academic reputation while resisting university attempts at adapting to the social and economic environment. In the 30 plus years since Duryea wrote these comments, it seems that departments have grown to the status of minicolleges in many ways. For example, university departments typically have their own personnel committees to deal with hiring and evaluating faculty, their own curriculum committees for approving new courses and degree requirements, their own grievance procedures for dealing with student and faculty misconduct, and their own secretarial and technical support staff. In more recent years, we see an increase in departmental advising centers (undergraduate and graduate program directors, included), websites, recruitment and marketing efforts, full-time staff to do placement and internship coordination, and even department chairs taking on more administrative functions such as fund raising and fellowship procurement.

Through the era of the late 1980s and 1990s, with the many phases of reorganization common in postsecondary institutions, budgets and functions became more decentralized to the department level, along with clear jurisdictions of influence and decision making emerging at many larger institutions. This strengthening of departmental authority also has given faculty more autonomy in the governance of academic functions, including establishing norms and operating values in line with, but somewhat independent of the larger institution (Tierney, 1989, 1999).

Crossing departmental lines, even to do team teaching, involves a new set of rules and negotiations that may make a rewarding experience a costly one. Part of this goes back to the well-developed administrative structure of departments that is far more recognizable today then it was 30 years ago. But other issues also arise with engaging in meaningful faculty work outside the unit. Going outside one's departmental home to work with faculty from other disciplines (departments) breaks the fundamental rules of the expert model in which individual research accomplishments are more highly valued than collaborative accomplishments. Interdisciplinary collaboration further challenges the reward structure predominately held dear by departmental colleagues. Crossing departmental lines requires faculty to redefine the nature of their work and may challenge the role they play in their home department.

Interdisciplinary collaboration requires participating faculty members to negotiate for release time, for credit for their work outside the home department, and for coverage of their responsibilities while they are "away" from the department. These negotiations take place both in and outside the home unit, with colleagues and with unit administrators. Depending on the interdisciplinary collaboration experience, whether it is teaching or research, the role faculty play and the expectations held for them become significantly altered. Both the home department and whatever interdisciplinary collaboration structure sponsors the project must reach an agreement on the altered faculty role during the period covering the assignment. These things are particularly true when describing interdisciplinary collaboration in the way we have done for this text.

Arrangements for role expectations such as receipt of student classroom or research credit hours and research overhead, modified performance review criteria, and even budget reallocations and procedures may be difficult to agree on and place participating faculty at professional risk if no agreements can be reached. Depending on the structure and culture of the departments, these negotiations may be made by administrators rather than faculty, as well.

For example, one of the most common forms of faculty collaboration is team teaching. This usually involves two or more faculty members from different disciplines dividing a course into separate parts in which each disciplinary approach to a problem or issue is presented. Team teaching often does not involve or require all faculty members to attend class at the same time, or develop the syllabus together. Instead, faculty usually break the semester down into equal parts and teach their section(s). It is less common for disciplinary approaches to meld together, for separate paradigms to be discussed or merged in the same discussion, and it is quite conceivable that no new way of thinking emerges from the experience for the students or the faculty. In a way, students just experienced two parallel constructions of the material without faculty facilitated synthesis. If the integration happens, it may occur outside the classroom, not as part of the intended outcomes of the faculty. Yet, even in this coordinated scenario, faculty need to negotiate roles, budget resource allocations, full-time equivalent student/faculty credit to their departments, and professional credit for offering the class. They have to establish how class evaluations will be interpreted in a standard class evaluation format that accounts for one instructor rather than two, and how those class evaluations will be used toward individual merit and annual reviews.

Such negotiations can be challenging, even when crossing role boundaries within a department. For example, with one's peers, does team teaching count as one half a class or a whole class when constituting teaching load? With decreased budgets leading to increased teaching loads on many campuses, this question may become more murky and problematic if the one-half class model is in use. Negotiations across departments for interdisciplinary collaboration efforts can be even more complex. We may assume that because all participants work at the same university, for instance, that the rules and definitions of work are the same. Yet, this assumption could just as easily be false, as it was for our research team.

Variation among departments in the way faculty "do work" are often not well understood by faculty outside the unit. These hidden variations may result in disadvantages to some faculty members while others may be advantaged by the same activities. Some faculty members may not be encouraged to participate in interdisciplinary collaboration if advancement and merit opportunities act as disincentives in one department and field, as opposed to another. Regardless of the nature of the relationship, it is important to facilitate an even playing field across departments in order to equally support faculty participation in interdisciplinary collaboration efforts. If we value this type of engagement, faculty must be allowed to renegotiate their roles when participating in interdisciplinary collaboration without risk to their careers or their home departments.

ALIGNMENT OF BUREAUCRATIC PROCESSES

One of the challenges of university partnerships is always the bridging of organizational structures across partners (Fairweather, 1988). We have already referenced the dilemma with how faculty construct work differ-

ently across units and the resulting expectations of their role, time allocation, and the like. There are other, more perfunctory bureaucratic and
structural components that also need to be addressed in faculty partnerships across multiple units. Most pressing, or obvious issues often have to
do with money.

In traditional consulting relationships, for example, contract arrangements are often limited to single units or even individuals. This simplifies
many management functions, such as budgeting and payroll, because the
contracting unit's administration systems dominate. When the partnership involves multiple units of the same institution, there are still myriad
management processes that need to be worked out in consort. Conflicting
management philosophies, processes, timetables, and personnel policies
all must be factored in. Departmental budgets can be cumbersome when
general funds are mixed with multiple sources of grant funds, course buy-
outs, and so forth. Faculty participation in interdisciplinary collaboration
efforts can further complicate a departmental budget, especially if carry-
over monies across term or fiscal year are ever involved. In many cases,
the role of the individual faculty member in course loads, advising, and so
forth, must be negotiated on a yearly basis. The multiple configurations
and multiyear nature of interdisciplinary collaboration activities can
require some percent of the departmental budget to be devoted to interdisciplinary collaboration efforts mixed with funds from other departments. They may require a reduced teaching load from the host
department for the interdisciplinary collaboration participant over multiple academic years. Or department funds may have to be made available
to support the faculty member until outside interdisciplinary collaboration money becomes available and can reimburse the department.

Of course, this plethora of funding scenarios is manageable and
becoming more common as resource bases shift and expand. Nevertheless, it adds to the complexity of maintaining a full and accurate accounting of departmental funds. If funds supporting the interdisciplinary
collaboration efforts are with agencies external to the university, accounting procedures and funding cycles are often different and at times, con-
tradictory. Issues such as the legality of sole-source funding of public
monies or even contract language often surface to delay anticipated
release of funds, causing some departments to gingerly balance or manipulate funds to cover what are believed to be temporary delays and shortages.

In the research team we studied, a disagreement over contract language among the partners delayed the release of funds for 6 months into
the project. During this time, the project administrator and others at the
university were involved in negotiating contract arrangements, trying to
align internal accounting processes with the stipulations of the external

contractor, and attempting to develop a level of trust and confidence with all parties. Departmental budgets and staff arrangements were held at bay during this period, in part because fiscal years were crossed and because it was not clear when the project budget would actually be finalized. This caused multiple departments to shift monies to temporarily account for the shortages. Some departments had resources to cover project involvement for the short run while others did not or were unwilling to do so.

The circumstances then, resulted in some faculty choosing not to participate in the project and others "volunteering" while trying to maintain their regular work expectations until support was clear. It also required a strong, top-down project leader to handle the bureaucratic and administrative functions that seemed stalled inside and outside the university. From a group development perspective, these delays and ambiguities did not encourage high levels of commitment and confidence in the project's potential success or the members' stability in working with it. Frustration and concern were outgrowths of this initial complication around the budget and fed into the tenuous group dynamics during early meetings of the team. The irony to us as researchers was that the funding source and fund recipient were both state agencies, yet behaved as totally separate and foreign agencies.

Another concern with departmental budgets and interdisciplinary collaboration efforts is how money related to such projects is funneled and to whom. Like most resources including individual research dollars, funding support for faculty participating in interdisciplinary collaboration efforts can become a source of political power and influence within the department or between departments. The one who controls the budget controls the resource base and the decision-making process (Morgan, 1999). This can influence the balance of power and paradigm dominance in favor of the department that controls the budget and the faculty member designated as "principal investigator" or "lead instructor." In order to reduce the opportunity for one department or discipline to have power and influence over another, we found it beneficial for interdisciplinary collaboration resources to be distributed through a neutral source. We discuss the idea of an organizational neutral space more fully later in this chapter.

Finally, we tend to think about budgetary procedures as interagency dilemmas when considering collaborative arrangements (Fairweather, 1988). Yet, we found that budgetary procedures often vary significantly between departments and colleges within the same university. Differences may be particularly acute between units housed within the traditional liberal arts disciplines and those considered "professional" disciplines because of institutional tradition, departmental evolution, and external funding streams. Spending limitations and ownership of equipment purchases may vary. Procedures to disburse funds may vary. Negotiated buy-out rates may differ, as likely do teaching and advising loads. Even how funds will be allocated and accounted for within and between departmental budgets may vary significantly. These differences between departments of participating faculty can greatly delay, if not sidetrack the progress of the interdisciplinary group as we found in our research team. It is important that these bureaucratic procedures align in order to fully support the faculty participants of interdisciplinary collaboration.

FACULTY REWARD STRUCTURES

In most research universities, and in Stage One behavior of our model, faculty are traditionally rewarded for their individual productivity. Sole authorship of publications based on a faculty member's own research and/or funded by external research dollars awarded to the principle investigator are valued more than co-authorship, co-investigator, or collaborative efforts. Under the traditional expert model, the criteria for tenure and promotion are based in large part on a faculty value system that rewards individual productivity and contribution to the field of study. The academic culture dictates much of the value system that under girds reward structures (Austin, 1990; Becher, 1989; Clark, 1987; Colbeck, 1998; Tierney, 1989) and we discuss this aspect in greater detail in the chapter on culture later in this text. We realize artificially separating structure from culture when discussing faculty rewards has its limitations. Yet, there are bureaucratic elements of faculty appointments, evaluation cycles, salary setting, and reward structure processes that affect interdisciplinary collaboration. We wanted to address these without attributing all of their construction to disciplinary culture. So we have opted for two discussions--one more administrative and the other, more cultural in nature.

Each year, faculty submit a portfolio or accounting of their productivity highlighted by the amount of research dollars they bring into the university, a list of articles and books published during the academic year, teaching evaluations, service to the community as well as a list of conference presentations completed. This portfolio of activity is then reviewed by a faculty committee within the department (or college, in smaller institutions) and an evaluation or assessment is given by the committee. While these criteria and process of annual reviews vary between universities and even departments within the same university, an equivalent value system is at work to answer the question, how productive has the faculty member been this year? An evaluation by peers remains the strongest factor in influencing decisions on tenure, promotion, and merit pay increases. This is true, regardless of the number of institutional review layers through which annual evaluations, merit ,and promotion criteria pass.

Faculty review committees have more difficulty in completing an assessment when publications are coauthored or research dollars are shared among other faculty and departments. Often, faculty are asked to state a percentage of individual work on coauthored publications, the role they played in the writing process, or the parts of the publication they were primarily responsible for writing. Faculty are also asked to designate who is the primary researcher on externally funded research both by the funding agency and the institution, and more "credit" acknowledged for this role. The number of identified coprinciple investigators are often limited by funding agents, attributable to more senior ranked colleagues, or designated to the unit through which the funds pass. This practice begins to illuminate some of the structural problems with evaluating individual accomplishments with coparticipants in an interdisciplinary collaboration. It gets messy and sometimes contentious, especially if rewards, resources, or release time are garnered by being the principle investigator. This is the practice of the traditional model and one that unfortunately, serves as a disincentive for interdisciplinary collaboration.

It is easy to see how participation in interdisciplinary collaboration efforts can challenge the traditional faculty reward system and render it extremely problematic in evaluating faculty productivity. Like Boyer's alternative forms of scholarship (1990), interdisciplinary collaboration efforts have some characteristics that are often considered unique when assessing faculty productivity. Those characteristics unique to interdisciplinary collaboration include time, perceived quality and type of publications, appropriate dissemination outlets, and who are the peer reviewers for interdisciplinary collaboration accomplishments.

Authors agree that collaborative efforts, including interdisciplinary collaborations, take time (Klein, 1990; Lattuca, 2002a; Salter & Hearn, 1996), for several reasons. We hold that interdisciplinary collaboration efforts take more time to develop than individual faculty research activity because of the need for cognitive integration and more team-like work orientations that are required if interdisciplinary collaboration is really to take place. Interdisciplinary collaborations are also likely slower to demonstrate outputs. Or perhaps more accurately stated, interdisciplinary collaboration efforts result in different forms of productivity than traditional refereed journal articles. The time cycle of interdisciplinary collaboration usually extends beyond the typical academic year, often without significant initial evidence of deliverables per se, specifically conference presentations, manuscripts submitted for publication, or written technical reports. The lengthier life cycle of interdisciplinary collaboration presents some problems for faculty release time, budgets and even performance review when the traditional model relies on an academic year cycle. These matters are not ameliorated when the funding cycle is a single calendar year, which runs counter to the academic year.

Faculty who participate in interdisciplinary collaboration efforts may therefore, be disadvantaged in tenure, promotion and merit reviews, and annual review cycles. Further, they may be penalized to the point of discouraging participation in interdisciplinary collaboration as well as to dissuade colleagues from considering participation in future interdisciplinary collaboration opportunities. Some of those considering participation in our research team, for example, were aware of past collaboration activities that had not gone well and had negative impacts on faculty who participated. As a result, they considered very carefully their own participation in the interdisciplinary collaboration we studied. Pretenure faculty and those still in the promotion cycle to full professor might be particularly disadvantaged by perceived "time lags," coauthored work, and nontraditional products and publishing outlets. Reviews of faculty productivity during the traditional academic year cycle may have to be more flexible in order to accommodate, support and encourage interdisciplinary collaboration participation. It might be wise for faculty to negotiate an understanding with the review committee in order to accommodate the review time cycle and criteria for evidence of scholarly productivity.

Alternative review periods such as multiyear evaluation cycles are often suggested when we talk about posttenure review because of the expectation that faculty work changes over the career, taking on various forms and extended-term projects (Baldwin, 1990; Licata, 1986). We propose that such considerations are warranted when looking at interdisciplinary collaboration and similar forms of scholarly engagement (Boyer, 1990) so that faculty are more confident to participate in this important work. Yet, an extended time cycle and alternative review criteria are only the beginning.

The question that is raised most often in the review process of interdisciplinary collaborative work is who should be the peer review group. A departmental committee, at times, becomes problematic as scholarly productivity of interdisciplinary collaboration typically extends beyond the disciplinary paradigms of department members. This may render traditional disciplinary standards largely unacceptable as evaluation criteria (Klein, 1990). In her research on collaboration, one of the participants in Gumport's study (1991) shared concerns about having her cross-disciplinary work fit into established review practices within her institution. The participant said, "It's harder to work when it's not fitting into your discipline in a particular way. You can't expect to get clear judgments and rewards, although you'll get different opinions about it.... The problem is the people who could judge it are out there and not in here in my department and my discipline" (p. 516). So how do faculty effectively evaluate multiple authorship of interdisciplinary collaboration scholarship? Further, how do they evaluate the quality of the journals that publish interdisciplinary collaboration work? Finally, how does one assess the level of contribution, either to the practical arena of scholarship or to the creation of new knowledge?

Clearly, the singular disciplinary lens does not provide the most appropriate judgment for interdisciplinary collaboration efforts. Nor are the publication outlets clear, because the issue of fit and judgment by reviewers of more disciplinary-based journal editorial boards is similar to those of more singularly focused disciplinary peer reviewers. Results of interdisciplinary collaboration research, by definition are not framed in discipline specific lenses or may not even necessarily conform to field specific conventions. This calls them into question in the minds of reviewers when looking for manuscripts that ascribe to more narrowly defined intellectual publication guidelines.

Even when more readily identified, some journals for publication of interdisciplinary collaboration research still lay outside the parameters of those defined as "premiere journals" in each faculty's members discipline and so the value given to these pieces may be less at evaluation time. It may be that peer evaluation and "high status" publication outlets must remain fluid, depending on the functionality of the interdisciplinary collaboration group. Or it may be that new, more project specific criteria are used to evaluate the utility of the scholarly products of interdisciplinary collaboration so that increased emphasis on impact of the work becomes important to peer reviewers. The intellectual needs of interdisciplinary collaboration review are discussed in more detail in the intellectual chapter later in this text.

We suggest that finding a set of interdisciplinary peers and using traditional criteria to evaluate faculty productivity in interdisciplinary collaboration participation remain some of the most crucial problems to be resolved in order to encourage and support interdisciplinary collaboration efforts (Gumport, 1991; Klein, 1990; Salter & Hearn, 1996). Without changes in the structural expectations, including evaluation criteria, only senior faculty, and probably a limited number of senior faculty at that, can afford to risk the career implications of regularly participating in interdisciplinary collaboration activities. This removes generations of young scholars from contributing to the interdisciplinary collaboration movement and working to develop creative new solutions to complex problems.

Clearly, a new organizational mindset and reward structure must be created in order to support and encourage interdisciplinary collaboration efforts. With this, we understand the need to cultivate different cultural norms and beliefs, as well. We do not advocate abandoning the traditional academic enterprise, but rather we support more active steps toward creating the changes Boyer (1990) and others suggested more than a decade ago, in this case, to support interdisciplinary collaboration. We believe universities will be more wiling to consider new models when interdisciplinary collaboration efforts are allowed to demonstrate a significant contribution to problem resolution and knowledge creation. The challenge for university leadership thus becomes creating an administrative structure that best encourages and supports interdisciplinary collaboration team efforts, budgets, incentives, and rewards across departmental lines. University leadership needs to be empowered to create new structures that are unencumbered by the rigid and bureaucratic departmental structures dominant on university campuses today. We believe this can effectively be accomplished by creating and sustaining a structural (as well as intellectual) neutral space on campus.

ORGANIZATIONAL NEUTRAL SPACE

Due to the power and influence that departmental affiliations often have over faculty work and expectations, it may be useful to develop an organizational structure that offers a "neutral space" from which to sponsor and support interdisciplinary collaboration efforts. We believe this kind of faculty work is better served when the administrative structure, budget and funding are removed from any one traditional academic department. Sponsorship through a department provides a political and power advantage of one discipline over another that causes dissonance in reconciling the knowledge engagement and disciplinary orientation issues of collaboration we have already identified. And, we believe that it creates severe impediments to the development of collaborative work engagements as suggested in our model. The strongest way to support interdisciplinary collaboration efforts is to create an organizationally neutral space through which the work is sponsored, nurtured, supported, and which is devoid of the political trappings of departmental or disciplinary association.

We make this recommendation in spite of the dilemmas we have already identified that occur when crossing structural lines such as negotiating load, salary, and so forth. We know that there are bureaucratic deterrents inherent in working across units that might be ameliorated, somewhat, by having a traditional department serve as the home of interdisciplinary collaboration. But from our research and the work of others studying cross-unit partnerships, we do not feel these benefits outweigh those accrued by depoliticizing the work as much as possible through the creation of a more neutral site for the interdisciplinary collaborative work.

There are a number of organizational models that universities have used to structure and sponsor interdisciplinary research over the last 30 years. Research institutes and research centers remain the most common formal structures within universities. Institutes and centers are often found at research universities and vary widely in their autonomy from disciplinary affiliations and sponsorships; they also differ in their degree of permanency. They provide a formal administrative structure to pursue external research funds and are usually supported to some degree by institutional resources, as well. Although many of these interdisciplinary institutes and centers have been affiliated with a discipline base at the point of their inception, more are, or have become independent from specific departmental association (Klein, 1990).

A matrix organizational structure has been another organizational configuration used for short-term sponsorship of interdisciplinary collaborations. Matrices are designed for specific purposes, often to allow bureaucratic organizations to respond creatively and more quickly, because of their ability to operate outside the formal structure of the university (Bolman & Deal, 1997; Morgan, 1999). But at the same time, matrices are not always afforded direct control of a budget, personnel decisions or evaluations, or other structural support mechanisms. In higher education organizations, matrices are also not typically expected to be institutionalized and made permanent. Doing so often leads back to the bureaucratic trappings that the unit was originally created to avoid, thereby lessening its effectiveness as a site of innovation and collaboration.

Organizational neutral space can be created through existing administrative structures that are devoid of specific disciplinary ties and perceived to be less political. Most universities have research or graduate school administrative structures. An organizationally neutral space could be created under this administrative umbrella. Some universities, particularly land grant universities and other public colleges have some form of outreach or community-based administrative structure that offers a more neutral space devoid of disciplinary ties. Budgets, procedures, contracts, and so forth, can all be initiated and executed through such existing structures to sponsor and support interdisciplinary collaboration efforts. Or a new office could be created under an existing structure. Not all participation issues for faculty are eliminated through these structural strategies, but many associated with the politics of money, credit, and work load negotiations may be more easily handled when it is not perceived that one academic unit is "winning out" over another.

In our research case study, an independent, university-wide outreach office was sponsored by the Provost's office with the mission of putting together teams of faculty to work on problems that communities in the state brought to the institution. The office provided administrative and leadership personnel to assemble faculty teams to address the outreach project we studied. There was never an intent for the office to sponsor only interdisciplinary teams. But over time, this organizational structure proved to be quite effective in pulling together faculty from a variety of disciplines without the departmental trappings of budget and sponsorship that tend to influence a dominant paradigm throughout the teams' work. This neutrality is a vital commodity in order for interdisciplinary teams to flourish.

Regardless of the specific configuration that is appropriate on a given campus, it is important that the sponsoring office or unit maintain its disciplinary neutrality to afford faculty maximum opportunity for participation. It is equally important that the office has the bureaucratic flexibility to act unencumbered by strict university policies and procedures that may be detrimental and counter productive to nurturing interdisciplinary collaboration initiatives. This may be more or less challenging to accomplish, based on the extent to which an institution's processes are centralized or decentralized. Depending on the way the university functions, it may be necessary to fund an administrative structure through private or unrestricted monies to free up and make the structures more flexible.

Perhaps the most important element to creating an organizationally neutral space is the administrative leadership. As we observed in our research team, leading an interdisciplinary collaborative team presents its own set of developmental challenges that may be more than those facing faculty group leaders generally. The leader has to be skilled in team development, contract management, conflict resolution, and so forth. But in order to facilitate the team's development along the three dimensions of the interdisciplinary collaboration model, the leader also has to be viewed as not advocating one disciplinary paradigm or departmental orientation over another. They have to be viewed by the interdisciplinary team as structurally and philosophically neutral, the same as those considering participating. A discussion of the leadership role is more fully developed in another chapter of this text.

SUMMARY

University organization, in particular traditional department structures with rigid disciplinary boundaries, tends to act as a barrier to establishing and encouraging faculty participation in interdisciplinary collaborations.

Faculty often do not have opportunities to interact intellectually with colleagues from other disciplines due to the physical isolation between different units on campus. The structures, timeframes, rules, and regulations that govern curriculum, program structures, committee organization, academic cycles, contracts, and faculty work in general also create separations and boundaries that are challenging to cross. They are time consuming to work through. These physical and bureaucratic separations allow faculty to further isolate themselves within their disciplines and behind their office doors, resulting in closer feelings and rapport with their disciplinary colleagues across the country than with their peers in the department across the hall.

Faculty participation in interdisciplinary collaboration also is inhibited by rigid departmental role expectations and budgetary inflexibility. Departmental policies and procedures that govern tenure, promotion, and merit pay tend to dissuade faculty participation, particularly among the junior faculty ranks who cannot afford to engage in "risky behavior" early in their careers. Participation in interdisciplinary collaboration efforts takes time often beyond the normal annual academic review cycles, and requires alternative role expectations that may strain departmental budgets. Involvement in interdisciplinary collaboration challenges the criteria for evaluating faculty productivity as the products are usually collaborative (instead of individual), take longer to complete, are typically disseminated in alternate formats, and raise the very real question of what peer group is appropriate to evaluate those products. Faculty should negotiate new role expectations and performance review criteria when they get involved in interdisciplinary collaboration activity. And those arrangements need to be formally sanctioned by university administrators and academic leaders.

Departments wield great power and influence in decision making that must be considered in sponsoring interdisciplinary collaboration efforts. We believe sponsorship is best served through an organizationally neutral space or administrative structure that has no singular department or disciplinary affiliation. The matrix organizational model works well in these situations where the interdisciplinary collaboration is viewed as a short-term, problem-based project with a recognizable ending period. Autonomous research institutes and centers, including outreach units, are better suited for more permanent activities and long-term projects. Such organizational structures must act to support neutrality for all disciplinary participants as well as provide for the administrative infrastructure necessary to carry out the interdisciplinary collaboration work.

In the end, depoliticizing the "disciplinary wars" and creating sufficiently flexible administrative and fiscal structures are key factors in facilitating effective interdisciplinary collaborations. While doing so does not resolve all the issues involved in bringing together faculty across disciplinary paradigms, the structural impediments to this kind of work are very real and need to be considered before faculty embark on the intellectually challenging work of integrative thinking and collaboration as we have defined it.

CHAPTER 7

INTERDISCIPLINARY COLLABORATION AND ACADEMIC CULTURE

Higher education institutions are known as normative organizations (Bergquist, 1992; Birnbaum, 1988), in which members are "ruled" through norms, values, traditions, and strongly held beliefs. In the instance of faculty, this organizational culture is typically moderated at least to some extent by the disciplinary culture with which one most closely affiliates. Distinctions have been made between "cosmopolitan" and "local" faculties whose allegiances and identities are more clearly defined through external agencies and internal agencies, respectively (Becher, 1989; Clark, 1987; Mintzberg, 1979). At the same time, most faculty can relate to multiple spheres of professional cultures that govern their work lives: the academic profession, the discipline, the academy as an organization, and the institution type (Austin, 1990; Clark, 1987; Masland, 1985). Each is present to one extent or another in the study we conducted, but our focus is particularly on the cultures of discipline and the academic profession.

Clark (1987, p. 7) has long grappled with the influence of culture on faculty and academic work. He describes disciplines as the "primary units of membership and identification within the academic profession." Disciplines are value-laden cultures, according to Clark (1963), that frame the beliefs and behaviors of faculty. They have their own traditions, social organization, reward system, professional status/dignity, and language (Becher, 1989). The disciplinary culture shapes assumptions about what is to be known and how, assumptions about the tasks to be performed and standards for effective performance, and assumptions about patterns of publication, professional interaction, and social and political status (Austin, 2002; Kuh & Whitt, 1988; Rice, 1998). Disciplines organize and concentrate experience into particular worldviews (Klein, 1990), and therefore, limit the kinds of questions asked, methods and concepts used, answers believed by faculty, and criteria for truth and validity. Once internalized, disciplinary culture becomes faith-like (Clark, 1963), often shaping faculty attitudes and behaviors without a real sense of consciousness or awareness. Becher (1989) calls these groupings the tribes of academe (p. 24), and his metaphor helps bring into focus the importance of disciplinary culture when discussing interdisciplinary collaboration.

Differences in disciplinary culture may be moderated, in part, by the strength of organizational culture. We would still expect to find at least some distinctions present even at small, liberal arts institutions where faculty may not be organized into departmental units. At these colleges, institutional culture is stereotypically quite strong (Birnbaum, 1988) and disciplinary culture, as a result, may be less compelling (Tierney, 1989). At complex research universities with diffuse institutional cultures, disciplinary differences might be particularly noticeable. Klein (1990) argues that, regardless of organizational culture, disciplinary structures are deeply embedded in any academic institution. Using cultural frames for analyzing faculty work and orientations to teaching and research illuminate variations across disciplines and professional areas (Austin, 1990; Becher, 1989), and help us understand some of the challenges faculty face with interdisciplinary collaboration.

DISCIPLINARY CULTURES AND STAGE ONE BEHAVIORS

Members on the research team we studied came to the project from several different professional and disciplinary backgrounds. Disciplinary orientations were often demonstrated through clashes of deeply held beliefs about ways to interact with communities, paradigmatic research differences in how to enact economic development activities, and principled disagreements about the value of alternative intellectual perspectives, collaboration, and outreach scholarship. As Parker Palmer describes, academic cultures build wide and high barriers between colleagues (1998), and this is what we found in the early months of the team efforts. For example, in reflecting on the early stages of the group's development, one member observed, "There were additional sources of conflict …

based on language and concept of group process." These differences were a function of the professional orientations of group members, reflective of their individual disciplinary training.

It was clear in the early stages of our study that the research team behaved in accordance with the norms to which members had been socialized and for which they were rewarded within the university and disciplinary system. Traditionally, university faculty are not collaborators as we define this because there is no strong incentive for them to be. Gumport (1991) notes that research university faculty are primarily oriented toward their discipline and their disciplinary colleagues. Faculty are acculturated to act independently and are primarily rewarded in annual evaluation, promotion, and tenure processes for scholarly products arrived at through rigorous, independent research. These are primarily single-authored publications in prestigious, selective journals (Bronstein & Ramaley, 2002; Fairweather, 1996; Tierney & Bensimon, 1996). Although faculty often work together in collegial, cooperative, or coordinated efforts, this typically means working independently on predetermined parts of the whole and then putting the pieces together. We thought of this traditional orientation toward working in groups as part of Stage One of our interdisciplinary collaboration model and found it was the way in which members expected to work when they first joined the project.

As faculty progress in their careers, they come to understand that certain kinds of work are valued more than others, often those that are more easily defined, quantifiably measured, and produced in a reasonably short time (Becher, 1989). This might be a function of their institution and its mission. It is just as likely an expectation of their field and disciplinary colleagues inside and outside of the institution. This disciplinary peer culture becomes a means of social coordination and almost coercive (Gumport, 1991). A strong culture keeps people in their assigned worldviews and penalizes those who stray from accepted community standards (Becher, 1989).

Evidence to support beliefs of what is most valued is often overwhelming, or perceived to be so. When faculty look closely at proposals accepted for conference presentations, manuscripts accepted for publication by review boards, and the foci of funded grant proposals, their beliefs are confirmed. Perception is also reinforced through the implicit and often untested interpretations of promotion and tenure decisions. We see who gets promoted and tenured, and make our own interpretations of factors that contributed to those decisions, often affirming the criteria we assumed was of value. For example, if we already believe publications in prestigious journals matter most, when a renowned scholar gets promoted, we do not question the other instructional and service contributions made but focus on the publication record as sole criteria in the decision. These convictions serve to reinforce our socialization and disciplinary training of what constitutes knowledge and what is really of value in faculty work. This is how meaning (values) is constructed and objectified.

Those involved in the research team we studied were conducting what some would call outreach scholarship or the scholarship of engagement (Boyer, 1990). This kind of work remains somewhat controversial in its definition and, particularly, in how it is assessed and valued across institutional settings. For example, outreach scholarship is often seen as important faculty work, but simultaneously as a detractor from the higher status activities of teaching and research. This continues to be the case even at those institutions with land-grant or community-based missions that purport the need to engage in this activity (Amey, 2002; Fear & Sandmann, 1997; Votruba, 1996). Credit for cross-disciplinary activity, multiple authorship, extended time projects with dissemination of findings in outlets atypical to the discipline, and so forth, can become points of dissention for faculty participants as they confront their colleagues in annual evaluations and promotion reviews. Faculty personnel committees shy away from activities less objectively evaluated and offer greater rewards to traditional research activities including refereed conference presentations and journal articles (Fairweather, 1993) and solo-authored publications. So work that spans disciplinary boundaries is less well understood and therefore, often rewarded differently than scholarship within the discipline that is single authored and published in sanctioned outlets. Further, activities in conjunction with public agencies or communities are often couched in terms of service, not scholarship.

In spite of the rhetoric surrounding scholarship reconsidered (Boyer, 1990; Glassick, Huber, & Maeroff, 1997), traditions within disciplinary cultures run high. These traditions largely stipulate what is of value, and therefore, how faculty will spend their time. The influences of disciplinary cultures also affect the way evaluation cycles are constructed at most institutions. The institutional processes often mirror the disciplinary biases against certain kinds of interdisciplinary work, including outreach scholarship and many forms of externally funded "team" activity. In a classic example of what we have labeled Stage One behavior, it becomes most expedient for faculty to select those activities that fit "neatly" into a single calendar or academic year whenever possible, since evaluative judgments on multiyear or extended term projects is quite subjective. In the case of the kind of interdisciplinary work we studied, the process time required for the members to move through the intellectual stages both could not be predicted nor fully controlled by the project administrator, or by the participating members. This leaves accounting in one's annual review portfolio for time spent in group norming (as opposed to product delivery) a challenge, for example.

As is true with so many externally funded grant activities, an embedded assumption seems to be either that teams are already in place having worked through Stage One and Stage Two processes or that the traditional Stage One "divide and conquer" work strategy yields the best results (Magolda, 2001). A common grant funding and subsequent work pattern seems to exist, regardless of its relation to reality. It consists of grant acquisition, start up functions, team formulation, task assignment, data gathering and analysis, and product delivery occurring within single funding cycles, often of a year or less. The end result is that the synergy of collaboration never gets a chance to develop, faculty remain largely unaffected in the reward structure since quality is often subjugated to quantity, and the utility of products delivered in this manner is left largely unassessed.

What we came to realize is that there are numerous ways institutions and departments culturally discourage, tacitly and overtly, the kind of collaboration studied here. We are not trying to divorce ourselves from the responsibility faculty have in creating the academic organizations in which they live, and which we critically examine here. But it is important to acknowledge that the disciplinary and academic cultures that we, as faculty, perpetuate and institutionalize in the forms of departments, reward structures, and professional organizations inhibit interdisciplinary collaboration. These value systems faculty have created and perpetuate hinder the very kind of intellectual work faculty profess to value.

Research on faculty and faculty work reiterates that institutional and departmental values and systems promote behavior reflected in Stage One of the model (dominant/expert/individual), and those relationships and activities with which we are most familiar in practice. They also promote behavior supported and reinforced by disciplinary cultures and the academic profession, writ large. Participating in alternate networks, such as interdisciplinary collaborations, when strong disciplinary orientations exist is a disincentive for faculty. This is especially true in environments with a real press to publish or perish, such as research universities (Gumport, 1991). Those who participate in interdisciplinary collaborations and other forms of voluntary faculty association do so at their own risk, Gumport suggests, by "leaping across the discrete departmental building blocks on which university organization rests" (p. 516).

There is some evidence from Lattuca (2002a) and others (Becher, 1989; Rice, 1998) that faculty may be more likely to venture beyond single frame thinking (the box) when they are in disciplines that have been, themselves, transforming. For example, in Lattuca's study of interdisciplinary faculty teaching, she notes one example of an individual working in the humanities who observed a general trend in her field toward more context-historical interdisciplinary approaches. As a result, this faculty member did not consider her own interdisciplinary engagement unusual. Cross-disciplinary activity may also be more common among fields that lack a clear sense of intellectual cohesion and identity (Becher, 1989). Becher uses geography as a case in point that adopts methods and concepts from other, related fields. In a different example, Lattuca interviewed a biologist working on global change issues who argued that forces outside the university, such as research sponsors required socially relevant and responsible projects. These external demands often fostered interdisciplinary science initiatives among faculty.

Although we did not find these same perspectives held by the faculty of our research team, we know of the national rhetoric suggesting the importance of collaboration, including initiatives by the National Science Foundation and other funders to encourage work across units and institutions in their calls for proposals and awarding of contracts. We do not suggest that imposed partnerships lead to integrated thinking, or that a project evaluator out of education necessarily collaborates interdisciplinarily with chemical engineers working on a funded project. But the requirement to work with researchers in other fields may provide at least an opportunity environment that can foster potential Stage Two and Stage Three activity among faculty. What is not clear, yet, is who chooses to participate in such activities. Nor is it clear to what extent interdisciplinary collaboration and other kinds of partnerships remain "add ons" to the more mainstream, single discipline-based research conducted by lone faculty members (Bronstein & Ramaley, 2002). For example, research university faculty, especially those in the tenure and promotion process, weigh carefully participation in activities that are more difficult to classify and evaluate within traditional reward structures (Blackburn & Lawrence, 1995). So, it remains to be seen if and how this same group chooses to get involved in interdisciplinary collaboration in spite of rhetoric and particular funding incentives.

A fundamental systemic, leadership, and policy shift seems required to accommodate alternate models to Stage One faculty work to any significant degree. The question arises then, how do we socialize faculty to work successfully in collaborative efforts, especially when these efforts require a different set of skills and experiences in order to be successful? We might also ask how do we, concurrently, socialize faculty to reward such efforts in merit, promotion, and tenure processes? And to honor this work in dissemination outlets, be they journals or conference presentations where peer judgments are involved?

CREATING CULTURAL CHANGE

Those who study culture of any kind understand the depth of its psychic embeddedness and the difficulty with creating cultural change (Kotter, 1996; Morgan, 1999). We believe, as do many others, that changing faculty culture is a similarly difficult challenge, yet one that is required if interdisciplinary work is really to be woven into the fabric of academic life. To create this change, in part, requires a deeper understanding of the forces through which culture is initiated and sustained.

Clark (1987), Klein (1990), Gumport (1991), Austin (1990, 2002) and others lay out foundations for using academic culture as a frame when examining faculty work. Building on their writing, sociocultural theorist such as Lattuca (2002b) help us understand more clearly the role of discipline, graduate preparation, and reward systems on faculty behavior in academic work. These factors, according to some sociocultural theorists, are cultural tools that moderate our experience in the world. We adopt and incorporate these cultural tools so that we may participate in particular social practices, including being a faculty member (Lattuca, 2002b). So if we approach the dilemma of how to change academic culture to better allow for interdisciplinary collaboration from this perspective, we have at least two powerful cultural tools on which to focus that reinforce disciplinary distinctions and behavior. The first is training during the graduate experience, when prospective faculty come to understand the norms, values, and "rules" of their respective disciplinary futures. The second cultural tool is university and disciplinary reward systems designed by faculty that adhere to and emphasize specific sets of cultural norms and values, often based on a particularly narrow set of sanctioned behaviors.

Graduate Student Training

Identification with the discipline begins with the socialization experiences of graduate school. It is during this indoctrination period that students learn the language, style, symbols, values, traditions, and folklore of respective disciplines as well as appropriate professional activities for the field (Austin, 1990, 2002; Becher, 1989; Golde, 1998). Wertsch, del Rio, and Alvarez (1995) suggest that socialization can be "viewed largely in terms of how tutees 'appropriate' the existing strategies of others and hence reproduce an existing cognitive and social order" (p. 16). Their definition certainly seems to apply to the explicit and implicit purpose of graduate education, especially in the preparation of future faculty.

Graduate students are trained to be experts on the cutting edge of increasingly specialized areas within their chosen discipline (Becher, 1989; Reynolds, 1992). This is especially true for those pursuing a doctor of philosophy degree, or its disciplinary equivalent, which is still held to be the more research-oriented terminal degree. As part of their education, graduate students are trained to debate and support their views through reasoned arguments grounded in the research literature. They are trained to become experts, as Palmer (1998) suggests, in programs whose intrinsic purposes are "so thoroughly to obliterate one's sense of self that one becomes a secular priest, a safe bearer of the pure objects of knowledge" (p. 100). Students learn to adopt a set of principles, tenets, and meaning structures of their chosen discipline through the intense socialization of graduate work (Dill, 1982). Through curricula, research, and other doctoral experiences, graduate student "apprentices" embrace a disciplinary context for their chosen profession that includes what questions are important, how work is done, and the relationship between teaching and research (Trower, Austin, & Sorcinelli, 2001). They learn which organizations "matter" in their field, the acceptance rates of prestigious journals, and the difference between high-end service and perfunctory professional tasks. These and other factors become driving forces in how graduate students come to see the academy, and perhaps the society in which it is located.

This socialization process is common across professions and certainly across the academy, even while the disciplinary orientations to which one is socialized can vary widely. For example, graduate students and new faculty in the humanities are socialized into an academic culture consisting of a structure of values, attitudes, and ways of thinking and feeling (Clark & Corcoran, 1986) that is quite different from faculty in the sciences (Kuh & Whitt, 1988). We are less concerned with these specific components of socialization in this discussion than we are with the process and its impact. Across graduate programs, the extent of this socialization process, if effective, is almost a form of hazing. The "pledge" (graduate student) internalizes these fundamental values and beliefs and they become part of the organizing process or lens used to view the world. In this respect, constructive/developmental theorists argue, the lenses cannot be critically examined because they are the frame of reference through which we create meaning; they are "subject" and are a subconscious part of us (Kegan, 1982; Kuhnert & Lewis, 1989). Playing this out in the life of those being socialized into faculty roles, graduate students (and early career faculty) are unable to reflect on these beliefs, lifestyles, and disciplinary cultures. In effect, developmentally, they *are* these beliefs. Not only have they acquired the technical expertise required of their field, but novice members have also adopted a "proper measure of loyalty to one's collegial group and of adherence to its norms" (Becher, 1989, p. 24). They are now "ready" to become a faculty member. Parenthetically, it is not until graduate students and early career faculty are able to distinguish themselves from their frames of reference that they are able to objectify and assess the work environment, career choices, and lifestyles they have adopted. It may be at this developmental juncture that they are actually cognitively able to participate in interdisciplinary collaboration.

Apart from indoctrination into the discipline, graduate school is about research skill acquisition and knowledge production particularly for those in doctoral programs. As graduate research assistants often witness firsthand, the research experience is typically an individual and specialized experience (Dill, 1982). Each doctoral candidate comes to know this deeply when completing their own dissertation research. Although peer writing groups may be used for support, collaborative research studies are uncommon dissertations in doctoral programs in many fields. Even in hard science degrees where lab data form the basis of the dissertation, students carve individual pieces of the research for their studies. Graduate students' immediate role models (faculty) demonstrate and enact this idiosyncratic experience (Nyquist et al., 1999) as they work toward tenure and promotion. This may be especially true for pretenure faculty, for whom the "lone scholar" remains a primary identity (Boice, 1992; Rice, 1998; Rice et al., 2000; Tierney & Bensimon, 1996).

These are the attributes of the disciplinary expert who views the world from the lens of a dominant paradigm, of a researcher most comfortable (or at least, most efficient) working alone, and a communicator who publishes his or her findings at the completion of the project in prestigious outlets. Learning is individualistic. Rewards are given for exemplary individual efforts. Graduate research training grants, dissertation research awards, and early career achievement recognitions are professional kudos given to individual scholars-in-training working on independent inquiry.

Historically in many fields, graduate school foundations and cultural traditions do not typically promote the attributes of, or valuing of, successful collaborators. We do not underestimate the importance of the individual interpretation of experiences. Nor do we negate the potential that any student may both learn the sociocultural norms of their discipline while choosing to discriminate the norms they will adopt and enact, and those they will not. Yet, it is impossible to deny the strength of this socialization process, the power structures that reinforce it (e.g., dissertation committees, professional references for employment, mentoring relationships), and the institutional and professional cultures that maintain it (e.g., reward structures, search processes, hiring criteria, promotion, and tenure processes).

From our research, we see the value in graduate students learning to work in nonhierarchical group settings, to communicate effectively within groups, and to be adaptable and flexible. For example, to value and promote different forms of faculty work such as Boyer (1990) advocated including interdisciplinary collaboration, perhaps graduate students would be better served to also learn how to listen, to recognize the weaknesses in their disciplinary paradigms, and to dialogue while they learn to debate. Finally, we advocate that graduate students would be positioned differently as future faculty if they learn the value of fostering a sense of community with their colleagues, and engaging in collaborative inquiry. Gaff, Pruitt-Logan, Weibl, and their associates (2000) suggest that faculty must be able to work collaboratively, as well as individually; this mindset and its practical foundations begin in graduate school. Such experiences can be built into the curriculum and pedagogy to enhance, not abandon, the existing graduate experiences.

At the same time, students must also see these behaviors in their faculty. As more skilled members of a culture or community, faculty play critical roles in mediating the learning of others (Lattuca, 2000a, 2000b). Lave (1997) notes, "Apprentices learn to think, argue, act, and interact, in increasingly knowledgeable ways, with people who do something well, by doing it with them as legitimate peripheral participants" (p. 19). This interdependent learning begins in graduate school and transcends that arena into the extended faculty career, drawing on different role models for inspiration, feedback, and learning.

Because there is significantly more research on early career faculty available, we chose here to emphasize graduate education and its role in creating cultural change toward the values inherent in interdisciplinary collaboration among prospective faculty. Of course, once on the job, as Boyer (1990), Dill (1982), Austin (2002) and others remind us, faculty continue to need socialization to the role, and to the academic and disciplinary culture within a specific organizational context. This includes values toward interdisciplinary collaboration and other "nontraditional" forms of faculty work. On-going socialization remains an important responsibility of senior faculty and other academic leaders, and a critical lever of cultural change.

Expanding the Culture of Faculty Rewards

In spite of our belief in the need to modify graduate student preparation, we remain convinced that faculty are successful in their disciplines and within the university because they are good at practicing what they preach. They are disciplinary experts, rewarded for expanding the knowledge of their discipline. They are rewarded for national recognition in their disciplines (Becher, 1989). They are heralded for being good at Stage One attributes in our interdisciplinary collaboration model. And as we have found, collaborative efforts take more time to be successful, often extend beyond traditional review periods, and contradict many of the Stage One expectations faculty bring to their professional lives. The level of activity including number of publications, research dollars, and so forth, also might be affected due to the level of effort required for collaboration. Faculty, in fact, may possess the attributes of Stage Two (cooperative knowledge engagement) or Stage Three (collaborative knowledge engagement) of the model. Yet, through traditional reward structures they have created themselves, research demonstrates clearly that faculty are rewarded most for practicing Stage One behavior (expert knowledge engagement).

In the case of the interdisciplinary collaboration project studied here, one participant captured part of the conflict between a Stage One reward structure and Stage Three engagement required for the project when observing,

> This university has a research agenda so naturally, you are going to get people who have to complete a research agenda. And they think that's their first primary goal. Well ... that can't be their primary goal for their work here on our team.... It may be something that they carry out, but they have to now carry it out under a community development agenda, which means that the community is involved in the design and the delivery of that research project. It doesn't mean that it doesn't get done. It means that the researcher is not the prime designer; he's got a team that includes the community.

This member saw the difference that deeper forms of collaboration entail and the potential conflict with the reward structure and perceived institutional mission inherent in choosing this path. She spoke to the kind of reorienting and expanding of academic culture that needs to be internalized for faculty to move from being "prime designers" and knowledge experts to team players. She identified some of the challenges that need to be addressed in order to infuse a collaborative culture into academic work.

The approach proposed for the project we studied was unique in several respects to the research traditions of many disciplines and likely, most university faculty. Although the effort was not entirely successful in creating a truly interdisciplinary experience, it did ask members to attempt to move beyond their personal research preferences and to explore the utility of interdisciplinary work and multimethod engagement/scholarship. For those who pursued their work in intellectual isolation, as they "had always done" research (typical of Stage One behaviors), the experience was often frustrating, limiting, and did not produce expected results. For those willing to work beyond their intellectual training and spheres, there was evidence of some degree of synergy, generativity, and a sense of collective pride in the outcome even if interdisciplinarity was not fully achieved.

Faculty disciplinary culture is created by and reinforced through the culture of the faculty reward structure just as the faculty reward structure is created by and reinforced through disciplinary cultures. Salter and Hearn question, "Are disciplines based on intellectual foundations that are simply recognized by administrative bodies, or does the institutional support for the organization of research and the universities into disciplines create the intellectual rationale for disciplines?" (1996, p. 20). In part, this "chicken or egg" debate only makes creating change in disciplinary cultures on behalf of interdisciplinary collaboration a much more challenging endeavor than changing the way we prepare future faculty. Some of these tensions were noted in the comments of our research team member above.

For interdisciplinary work to become more common, institutions and faculty within them need to cultivate a different kind of research culture (Boyer, 1990; Ramaley, 2000; Votruba, 1996). As apprentices, graduate students need to learn that the implications of research, including interdisciplinary research, are as important as the rewards derived from publishing results (Fairweather, 1996). Fairweather suggests that redefining research requires expanding the acceptable forms of research productivity beyond refereed articles and books (p. 197), and we would add, beyond discipline-specific journals. If the root premise of supporting interdisciplinary academic work is correct in that it likely yields more innovative and consequential results for complex problems (Klein, 1990; Salter & Hearn, 1996; Sandmann & Flynn, 1997), then it represents a move toward assessment of scholarly impact rather than only volume. This is likely to result in a more labor-intensive evaluation process for faculty, because simply counting publications, presentations, and grant dollars will be insufficient assessments. But without such differences in accounting for work, little change can be expected. In many ways, interdisciplinary collaboration and a focus on impact results in research for the public good (Fairweather, 1996). Room in the traditional academic culture needs to be made for this, just as it does for technology transfer and outreach scholarship.

As noted, there can be difficulty in distinguishing and "accurately" measuring individual contributions in a collaborative effort (Foster-Fishman & Stevens, 2002). Models to do so are unusual in many disciplines, not to mention the need to find university-wide acceptance for those measures when they exist. Where models for evaluating collaborative work or networks of "peer reviewers" for such work exist, gaining acceptance for these evaluations and rewarding collaborative work that is not disaggregated to individual contribution is a challenge still.

We realize that some disciplines have schema for evaluating and assigning contributions to multiple authored publications. For example, hard science fields often follow a model of including the principle investigator(s) on articles or presentations. In other fields, faculty spend time discriminating first from second authors' contributions, conceptual ideas from data analysis, junior members from senior scholars, and so forth, in order to distinguish individual effort for the sake of the standard means of assessment. None of this accurately reflects real interdisciplinary collaboration, even though it may account for cooperative work. It is ironic that in institutions whose primary missions are the discovery of knowledge, avenues to discovery, such as collaboration, are systemically discouraged. Instead, even when alternate forms of scholarship are accepted, we still insist on identifying singular contributions of faculty partners. In the end, for many, the challenge to pull apart the integrated learning of an interdisciplinary collaboration effort is antithetical to the work. The paradox of making truly integrative and collaborative work fit neatly into traditional boxes becomes another time consuming and often futile endeavor. Focusing on traditional Stage One publications becomes a more straightforward approach to academic work.

Truly internalizing the message that the academy and one's field value interdisciplinary collaboration requires many cultural changes. Graduate students and early career faculty need to see that their more senior faculty colleagues are rewarded for this kind of work, rather than penalized or delayed in the promotion and reward structures. Similarly, messages are conveyed in hiring processes that clearly set the stage for pretenure faculty behavior around issues of collaborative research. Different messages have to be communicated that demonstrate the value of this work even during interviewing for positions. Hiring criteria are especially important in comprehensive and liberal arts colleges, where survey data show that faculty socialization is a major factor in faculty research behavior (Fairweather, 1996). But all participants in a search process come to understand what is of value in the design and implementation of interview protocol and campus visits, as well as selection criteria that drive decisions. If perception is reality, the implicit messages conveyed during faculty search activities reinforce certain cultural values to another generation of graduate students and pretenure faculty. The role of academic leaders in shaping cultural understandings is critical, whether they be senior faculty, department chairs, or academic deans. Leaders need to help expand and reconstruct the current definitions of research to include more forms of scholarship (Boyer, 1990; Foster-Fishman & Stevens, 2002; Glassick et al., 1997), including interdisciplinary collaboration, and be sure this work is clearly and equitably rewarded.

MATRIX ORGANIZATIONS AND CULTURAL DILEMMAS

The research team we studied was situated largely outside the traditional organizational structure of its research university. We contend that this may often be the case when interdisciplinary work is underway, or at least should be the case. We described the structural aspects of matrix organizations in the chapter dealing with other organizational issues, but there are also cultural aspects of this configuration relevant to interdisciplinary collaboration and teams worth discussing. Whether deemed a true matrix organization defined in organizational terms or not (Morgan, 1999), the cultural dilemmas for the interdisciplinary team may be similar to those of organizational groups brought together for certain projects that are not intended to become institutionalized such as task forces or project teams. Such groups form without many of the institutional formalities characterizing departmental structures. Tierney (1999) calls these "soft project structures" (p. 38), and sees them as key configurations that allow for creativity, innovative responses, and that can minimize the traditional press for power and authority among traditional administrative units. This is simultaneously an advantage and a curse.

The advantage comes with the opportunity to create a culture outside the traditional trappings of which we have been critically mindful throughout this text. It is conceivable for the matrix organization (and other soft project structures) to establish its own culture, norms, values, ways of working, language, and so forth, that bring out the best in members rather than hold them accountable only to the ideologies of their respective disciplinary homes. Of course, the reality is that members live simultaneously in both the world of the matrix and of their home units. The pressures of the disciplinary homes, exercised through rewards, budgets, support staff, graduate student availability, and so forth, often override the benefits of an interdisciplinary culture developed in a matrix organization. Faculty who work in interdisciplinary collaborations may feel marginalized, like second class citizens in the academy because of efforts to maintain two cultural identities. Even if the matrix develops a strong culture within itself, if the larger institution does not value the interdisciplinary collaboration, or the matrix structure, faculty commitment to the work will be seriously tested as they try to straddle conflicting cultures.

It is also true that creating a self-contained culture is a leadership challenge, especially under the time constraints usually inherent in this kind of work or when the leader is associated strongly with a particular cultural orientation. Even when relationships are intended to be in place for longer periods of time, as with interdisciplinary degree programs for example, there still is a lengthy developmental process that the group goes through to establish a sense of culture and collective awareness. In situations with fixed time parameters, the impetus to take on this task may not be strong. In both scenarios, looking for and creating opportunities to reinforce shared values, norms, behaviors and beliefs are key leadership challenges and strategies. Utilizing cultural artifacts to enhance a sense of connectedness, identity, and enthusiasm for work requires regular attention and an appreciation for the importance of this often subconscious organizational functioning. For example, in the research team we studied, the project leader took opportunities early in the group's development to celebrate small accomplishments in an effort to instill a sense of collective ownership of and pride in the work among members.

All of the challenges associated with collaboration we have noted require expanding traditional cultural definitions and parameters if initiatives like interdisciplinary collaboration are to take hold in the academy. Interdisciplinary collaboration efforts have the promise of expanding knowledge and its utility to societal problems, but affect the cultural strongholds of the disciplines long associated with faculty work and identity. So change may be slow and difficult.

SUMMARY

Researchers and practitioners have long grappled with the influence of culture on faculty and academic work. They agree that disciplines are value-laden cultures that frame the beliefs and behaviors of faculty. At complex research universities with diffuse institutional cultures such as the site of our research team, disciplinary differences might be particularly noticeable. Using cultural frames for analyzing faculty work and orientations to teaching and research illuminate variations across disciplines and professional areas, and help us understand some of the challenges faculty face with interdisciplinary collaboration.

Most research on faculty and faculty work reiterates that institutional and departmental values and systems promote behavior reflected in Stage One of our interdisciplinary collaboration model (dominant/expert/individual), and those relationships and activities with which we are most familiar in practice. Participating in alternate networks, such as interdisciplinary collaborations, when strong disciplinary orientations exist is a disincentive for faculty. Understanding more clearly the role of discipline, graduate preparation, and reward systems on faculty behavior in academic work is important to creating cultural change that supports interdisciplinary collaboration.

Since significantly more research on early career faculty is available, we chose to emphasize graduate education and its role in creating cultural change toward interdisciplinary collaboration among prospective faculty. We suggest socializing graduate students to equally appreciate interdisciplinary collaboration and other "nontraditional" forms of faculty work in addition to the traditional research activities to which they are typically well indoctrinated. This is not an easy change given the current faculty role models from whom graduate students learn their craft.

Faculty disciplinary culture is created by and reinforced through the culture of the faculty reward structure just as the faculty reward structure is created by and reinforced through disciplinary cultures. For interdisciplinary work to become more common, institutions and faculty within them need to cultivate a different kind of research culture. Graduate students and early career faculty need to witness senior faculty colleagues rewarded for this kind of work, so they believe in its institutional and disciplinary value. Changing messages conveyed to graduate students and early career faculty during faculty search activities can reinforce a more inclusive set of cultural values about forms of research and collaborative work.

Although not a panacea for facilitating interdisciplinary collaboration, innovative organizational structures that can develop their own cultures, such as matrix organizations, may be beneficial. One result of this strategy is that faculty will be straddling multiple cultures that will sometimes conflict. The extent to which this is personally and professionally too great a challenge will inevitably affect participation in interdisciplinary collaboration. Without these organizational configurations, however, we already see involvement diminished.

Interdisciplinary collaboration efforts hold the promise of expanding knowledge and its utility to societal problems, but affect disciplinary cultures that define faculty identity, faculty work, and reward structures. Cultural change is seldom easy and rarely quick but methods exist to do so through creative leadership and committed faculty.

CHAPTER 8

THE INTELLECTUAL PROCESS

Learning Integrative Thinking in Interdisciplinary Collaboration

When studying faculty, we often focus on demographics, productivity (Blackburn & Lawrence, 1995; Fairweather, 1993, 2002), careers (Baldwin, 1990; Baldwin & Blackburn, 1981), tenure (Tierney & Bensimon, 1996), and similar topics. It is far less common to consider how faculty learn or come to learn, and how that learning affects their work (Lattuca, 2002a, 2002b; Neumann, 1999; Weiland, 1994), although similar studies of professionals' learning are common among adult educators (e.g., Mezirow, 1991; Mezirow & Associates, 1990; Palmer, 1998). In studies of college students, by comparison, we have long understood that cognition and context are inextricably intertwined and considerable time has been spent researching various configurations of these relationships (e.g., Baxter-Magolda, 1992). The difference between research on students and research on faculty might be explained through the ability to use a learning lens. To study faculty work as a learning enterprise requires us to separate ourselves from our work and to internalize the subject in order to see the object (Kuhnert & Lewis, 1989). We have to make conscious that which is normally quite subconscious or perhaps even unconscious—our learning processes.

Breaking Out of the Box: Interdisciplinary Collaboration and Faculty Work, 95–109
Copyright © 2004 by Information Age Publishing

What we have come to believe through this study is that interdisciplinary collaboration as a form of faculty work is really a process of learning, and that leadership in such a context is really about facilitating faculty learning. If we think about interdisciplinary collaboration as, fundamentally, a form of individual and collective learning, we need different ways to conceptualize, study and interpret this interaction than those lenses often associated with studying faculty work. Framing our understandings through learning theories seems a productive way to go, whether these are individual learning theories and/or organizational learning theories.

SOCIOCULTURAL PERSPECTIVES AND TRANSFORMATIONAL LEARNING

In support of this interpretation, Lattuca (2002a, 2002b) describes a number of learning theories that shed light on the social and contextualized nature of learning (e.g., Forman, Minick, & Stone, 1993; Greeno, 1997; Lave, 1997; Lave & Wenger, 1991; Rogoff, 1995). These theorists purport that learning cannot be understood apart from its historical, cultural, and institutional contexts, and use labels such as sociocultural theory, situated cognition, and situated learning to describe their concepts. They argue that cognition (learning) is a social process rather than an individual one. Instead of looking at learning as solely an individual activity removed from the setting in which it takes place, sociocultural theorists see social and cultural activity as the fundamental basis for learning and the context as an integral part of learning. Vgotsky (in Wertsch, 1985) posits that one cannot understand the individual without first understanding the social context in which individuals exist. Lave and Wenger (1991), laying out the precepts of situated activity, offer that knowledge and learning are relational in nature. Context is an important factor and meaning is a negotiated construct. Lave and Wenger contend that learning is a process of integration into a community of practice. In thinking about the original motivation for participating in the interdisciplinary team that we studied, one participant seems to speak directly to these ideas of community engagement, learning, and the social context when he said, "[The collaboration project] combines all of the issues, personal and professional that I'm interested in working on at the moment. Shifts in theory, the application of research in the lived environment. Across disciplinary work, where you take different expertise and points of view and background and try to integrate it. Group process operations, group decision making patterns, I'm very interested in systemic change."

Minick, Stone, and Foreman (1993) suggest that interpersonal relationships in the course of shared activity in a particular institutional context are critical to learning. Translating this to our study, we found that the interactions during the attempt at interdisciplinary collaboration were critical to individual and collective learning. It was through these inter-personal relationships, when paradigms were discussed and ideas shared that learning took place, allowing the team to move along the three dimensions of our model (disciplinary orientation, knowledge engage-ment, and work orientation). The emphasis on the collective or group, then, seems useful for helping to more deeply understand the intellectual learning component of interdisciplinary collaboration and critically examining the ways in which individuals and their contexts interact. To understand how faculty learn to do interdisciplinary work, we have to look at the cognitive processes that allow faculty to think interdisciplinary ideas. We also need to examine how this learning is accomplished through social interactions with others and with the tools of different communities of practice (Lattuca, 2002b).

Although colleges and universities may develop structures, policies and even cultures that provide incentives and opportunities for interdiscipli-nary research and teaching, this way of working requires a prior step. Fay (1987) observes that ideas are a function of social conditions, but they play a causal role in creating and sustaining particular social structures (in Smyth, 1989, p. 184), including groups, teams, and collaborations. Before they are likely to take advantage of said structures and policies, create such cultures, or even see the need for and value in them, faculty have to undertake a form of learning that allows them to engage in interdiscipli-nary collaboration. Lattuca (2002a) calls this learning the imaginative work of interdisciplinarity. Others would couch this learning in adult development terms (Kuhnert & Lewis, 1989; Mezirow & Associates, 1990). We saw this learning as the continuum transitions of knowledge engagement (ways of connecting to knowledge) and of disciplinary orien-tation (lens through which one views the world). One team member described the transition process this way:

> We need to get better at how all of us integrate new knowledge. And the critical issues of how you move from what our current beliefs are...this is complicated. Everybody goes through at least three steps as they change their point of view. And that is, first you have to understand, that we have to understand there is a problem with what we are currently doing. Secondly, we have to understand that there is a new way of doing it. And better in some fundamental way. Third, we have to practice it and fourth, we have to integrate it. And in many ways, we are at the point where we are practicing new behaviors in this process. We haven't, not all of us including me, have integrated it all.

Moving from a focus solely on the individual to the sociocultural set-ting in which learning is embedded, as advocated by theorists like Lattuca (2002a, 2002b), we more closely examine structures and interrelations within communities of practice—in our case, the interdisciplinary research team. What we found was not unexpected from a sociocultural perspective. Individual members of the research team evolved over their time together, having been influenced, affected, and in some cases, trans-formed by and through their interactions with other members of the team. Without always labeling it as learning, with a capital "L," many members spoke of ways in which their thinking was being informed, altered, and adapted as a result of the views of others. The extent to which these new ideas were internalized, and therefore, learned, might account for the transition through the three stages we used to artificially differen-tiate our interdisciplinary collaboration model on the continuum of disci-plinary orientation.

INTERDISCIPLINARITY AS TRANSFORMATIVE LEARNING

Improved research practice in higher education is a collaborative and dia-logical process in which, Engestrom (1999, in Lattuca, 2002b) notes, "dif-ferent perspectives and voices meet, collide, and merge" (p. 382). These viewpoints, orientations, ideologies and language are deeply rooted in different disciplinary communities and in different disciplinary practices. As one member of the research team shared,

> We are struggling with some very fundamental differences in philosophy approach, historical practice, personalities, and we are trying to make changes in some of the most ingrained personal senses ... and it is extraor-dinarily difficult to do. So we are dealing with some real fundamental stuff here that by its nature is horribly difficult to make a difference. And person-alities always make a difference in that. In some ways, I'm not sure we know enough to do it well. The amount of time it takes, the amount of energy and the amount of knowledge is a horrible limit on this. And that's tough to establish real trust between human beings. It is a hard process. So I think we are always at risk of not being able to pull this off.

These differences can continue to coexist within a collective activity, which was part of what we labeled coordinated knowledge engagement in Stage Two of our interdisciplinary collaboration model. But a truly shared understanding of a problem comes for us in Stage Three of our model. This is a collaborative and analytic achievement (Engestrom, 1999) repre-senting a higher cognitive developmental plane. This may be rare in the academy and certainly, is not to be taken for granted. Engestrom and others argue that the task of problem construction is critical to innovative learning and new knowledge, yet one we would argue is often bypassed when faculty come together to work. Typically, faculty work on projects takes one of two approaches. It may be structured hierarchically, such as a senior/junior mentoring relationship or senior researcher working with a research associate. Another common approach to faculty working together is to dole out responsibilities intending they be brought back to a senior analyst for compilation, which is what we have called cooperation. In either case, the problem construction is less often a collective activity but is assumed to be the responsibility of senior colleagues, knowledge experts, or the designated leader of the group. It is not the more authentic collaboration of intellectual peers where shared understanding underpins the activities referenced in sociocultural theory.

One of the persons involved in the original conception of the interdisciplinary collaboration effort we studied was privy to earlier attempts by the university at "multiprofessional and transdisciplinary" work. Her multiple experiences with these efforts led to the following observations before joining the research team we studied:

> There were common problems, it seemed to me, in all these organized efforts. Academic domain was a primary issue; ultimately, people could not surrender their own prevailing paradigms and structures for problem-solving. Too many people were involved in project conceptualization, and often, they were not the individuals who would be expected to do the work. In the project conceptualization phase, struggles ensued over language, theory, relevant literature, outcomes, and interventions. These struggles were resolved by waves of revision in project proposals, with the project either a passionless, vague political compromise or the triumph of one perspective over another with subsequent diminished participation by the disenfranchised groups. Planning committees were polyglot in composition, reflecting both those groups who had genuine interest and those whose presence were being courted for other reasons. Expectations for outcomes to be produced were excessively high, perhaps because there was a sense that the programs were drawing from the breadth of the entire university. Finally, multidisciplinary projects were typically not well-related to the traditional mission of academic units on campus and therefore, to some degree, lacked internal administrative support from chairs, directors and deans. In short, multidisciplinary projects were not particularly collaborative, took too much time to plan, excluded ideas from those not sharing a dominant paradigm, promised too much, and often left participants marginalized even within their own academic units.

Her reflective comments illustrate the range of interdisciplinary collaboration issues across the myriad aspects we have examined. They represent some of the cognitive and learning challenges faculty face when trying to work through multiple disciplinary orientations and in trying not to remain in Stage One thinking. The challenges she articulates also speak clearly to why, in many instances, faculty work continues to follow the expert, individualistic model and does not move far beyond that approach.

Intellectual Neutral Space

As the members moved through Stage One of the team development process we studied, and its sundry conflicts and paradigmatic frictions, we found faculty needed a safe space to explore issues and to consider the merits of other disciplinary perspectives. We have labeled this "intellectual neutral space." Adopting respect for and an open mind to alternatives is necessary for the transition from Stage One (competing perspectives) to Stage Three (adoption and internalization of complementary perspectives); it is requisite to integrative thinking. As Palmer suggests (1998, p. 106), "we cannot know ... if we stand only in our own shoes." To achieve interdisciplinary collaboration and integrative thinking, we have to have opportunity to see from another's perspectives in an environment where we are not penalized by doing so.

Faculty function within meaning systems (Mezirow & Associates, 1990) largely shaped during graduate study and cultivated through the discipline. Depending on the discipline, we might call these meaning systems by one of several labels: "lenses," "frames," "orientations," "paradigms," to name a few. These meaning systems provide a complex network of beliefs, psychological assumptions, and theories that help us understand life around us (Clark, 1963, 1987). They act, sociocultural theorists purport, as filters and lenses of meditation and interpretation for us. As we have discussed, in addition to acting as organizing systems, these filters often establish "habits of expectation" (Mezirow & Associates, 1990) that distort or limit our perceptions. Senge (1990) and other organizational theorists call these frames of reference "mental models" and cognitive maps. To develop intellectually in terms of knowledge engagement and discipline orientation, one has first to make conscious the mental models and disciplinary paradigms that often function below our level of awareness yet guide our behavior and affect our decision making (Kegan, 1982; Kuhnert & Lewis, 1989). Then, one has to be willing and able to attend to, and later incorporate the cultural filters, mental models, and disciplinary paradigms of others. One has to be willing and able to learn.

For our research team, intellectual neutral space at times really meant more than just the freedom to explore the ideas of others without penalty. In a way, it could be characterized as an "intellectual demilitarized zone," a holding pattern (Heifetz, 1994), or a kind of developmental moratorium. It was a break in the verbal sparring and disciplinary posturing that foreshadowed the emergence of shared understanding. The neutral space afforded the exploratory venue through which faculty were able to listen, to posit ideas, to suspend paradigmatic presumptions, and to begin to really adopt and internalize the disciplinary orientations of others. The break provided opportunity for dialogue in the true sense of Senge's (1990) term.

In the group we studied, neutral space was represented by a particular point in time when the tenor shifted and members began to speak more directly about the needs of the constituents they were trying to serve. Every member of the team clearly described this particular transformative moment. It was not a conscious choice of group members to suddenly begin talking in the third person and orienting their comments from the perspective of the community they were supposedly trying to help. However, the tensions caused by the regular disciplinary clashes that were a function of attempts at collective work and hierarchical posturing seemed to subconsciously push the members toward some kind of safe haven. For most of Stage One of their interactions, members could not resolve their cognitive differences, and as individual power brokers, were unable to successfully co-opt the group to any singular approach or way of thinking. Few alternatives were left to them than to call a kind of intellectual truce—a pause in the fighting, so to speak.

As noted, the truce was not a conscious one at first or one intentionally established to move members to another intellectual plateau. Rather, it seemed similar to the teachable moment about which we speak in faculty-student classroom interactions. And at that moment, faculty focused on ideas that did not represent the disciplinary orientations of any of them. A kind of synergy or generativity resulting from weeks of talk erupted, allowing the emergence of ideas informed by many perspectives but "copyrighted" by none. In this way, the language for the ideas was also not politically charged, and could be critically examined and later owned by all members of the team.

This transformational thought process was not expected by members or planned by the project administrator. Yet, in reflecting on their experiences with the team, every member pinpointed the same moment, concept, and language that marked this transformation. It remained clear even months later. As one person recalled, "[Finding the neutral space and using it in common], maybe that's part of this shift from parallel perspectives to integrative ones. We're developing more of a common language."

What is not as clear to us as observers or to the team members themselves is whether this intellectual neutral space could be intentionally created or its timing anticipated. There is no question of its importance to the interdisciplinary collaborative process, and how differently things were afterwards. Perhaps intellectual neutral space is central to overall interdisciplinary collaboration in general; it certainly seemed key to team development. Being aware of the potential need *for* intellectual neutral space, and knowing how to interject or create this space is a valuable leadership lesson. How the latter occurs is something we can posit but not something we know for certain. In this regard, we mirror those who have stumbled across this particular organizational and group dynamic need in the past but who have not been able to precisely denote whether it is administratively manageable, a natural artifact of group development, or other such explained phenomenon.

Dialogue

Arriving at shared understanding even if members think it is important requires time—time for the collaborative and dialogical process to unfold. This makes the idea of truly collaborative efforts slower than individual scholarly activity. Rarely in higher education do we find that sufficient time is afforded for anything, let alone to develop genuine understanding through dialogue. Although business and the private sector advocate and have adopted, for example, ideas of dialogue (Senge, 1990, 1996, 1998) and learning organizations (O'Banion, 1997) more frequently than postsecondary education, closer examination often reveals high rhetoric and low organizational learning across sectors.

In higher education, there are many structural factors that discourage dialogue as Senge (1990) defines it. Bureaucratic elements of the academic calendar truncate and seem to dictate aspects of potential collaboration and decision making. For example, courses being scheduled a year in advance or more inhibit the time required for designing and accommodating truly collaborative learning experiences for students whose programs of study often hold no space for new (and late developing) initiatives. Academic years that run counter to calendar years or to fiscal years of funding agents cause quick start-ups to be the rule in grant and contract research activity. Who has time to listen, discuss, and learn from others when the clock is ticking on research deliverables almost before the ink is dry on the contract? At the same time, faculty from different disciplinary orientations seem to be adept at working in coordinated fashion (parallel play) on a project that allows them to meet stated deadlines, produce deliverables, and deliver forms of tag-team teaching. Do these manifestations of work equate to interdisciplinary collaboration? We would say no.

For reasons stated, and many more, academics often do not engage in the dialogic processes required for real collaboration, including laying aside knowledge biases and right answers (Senge, 1990) so that new interpretations are possible. It is unlikely that most faculty will lay aside all discipline-based assumptions, although they can suspend them as Senge suggests and hold them up for examination and scrutiny. This makes it possible to establish an environment where dialogue is accommodated to a greater extent than the win-lose positional bargaining (Morgan, 1999; Scott, 2002) that tends to dominate group behavior. As the team moves along the dimensions of Stage Two, faculty develop beyond mere tolerance of each other, which might have characterized the feelings of many in Stage One. We saw the complexity of intellectually-bound relationships developing in that even though parallel paradigms were accepted, members were still exploring for deeper understanding. They were not trying to eradicate their differences but were trying to embrace and understand them (Tierney, 1994). They were doing so within the rhetoric of academic collegiality and the expectation of some professional civility. In such environmental contexts, Klein (1990) notes that premature closure for the sake of amity is often an artifact of early collaborations but that this "illusion of friendship" (p. 122) can be costly when it inhibits more genuine understandings and common language. "In their anxiety about easing tensions, [faculty] may avoid the very complexity on which ultimate success may depend." Palmer (1998, p. 151) calls this convention "making nice" with each other, feigning collegiality in a way, and sees the practice as a critical inhibitor to developing dialogue and genuine understanding.

When studying our research team, we found that moving along the developmental continua of knowledge engagement and discipline orientation required a form of learning that involved, "listening to the experiences of others, promoting a capacity for self-criticism, and using such criticism as the basis for developing programmatic discourses for building alternative hopes and realizable visions" (Giroux & Freire, 1987, p. xii). We speak of dialogical methods of teaching that engage faculty and students in a joint search for knowledge (Smyth, 1989). Similarly, interdisciplinary collaboration is rooted in a dialogical method of inquiry that engages multiple parties in a joint search for knowledge and common understanding. It is, again, a social process (Lattuca, 2002b; Mezirow, 1991; Smyth, 1989; Wertsch, 1985) where understandings are arrived at through negotiated and shared means (Smyth, 1989).

Actively engaging in dialogue, rather than debate, provides the means for listening to the perspectives of others but also the "truce" time for self-reflection required of learning. Discourse is reflection made public, and is required for a learning transformation (Clark, 1963). Changes in meaning structures, including disciplinary orientations, rely on critical reflection (Mezirow & Associates, 1990). Through this reflective process, underlying assumptions of the discipline perspective are identified, critically assessed, and reshaped to allow for the development of broader, more inclusive meaning structures (Clark, 1963; Kuhnert & Lewis, 1989). The project administrator of our research team tried to build opportunity for reflective time and paradigm exploration into the meeting schedule. She saw the importance of thinking time to the overall process she was trying to facilitate, and articulated her view of the impact as, "This time seems to be what is allowing the team culture to develop, letting ideas be tossed out and discussed, for letting people do more than a check listing of tasks but to be more reflective and accepting of the process." Since change is often not revolutionary for faculty, but evolutionary, it may begin similarly to what we saw in the processes experienced by our research team.

As dialogue took hold, team members began to accept others' perspectives as legitimate even without owning them personally, or allowing them to truly permeate their meaning structures. This process of seeing *from* the lenses of others was a hallmark of Stage Two in our model. Members of the team accepted the validity of ideas generated by others, although they did not always internalize those ideas themselves. This might be characterized as reciprocal learning (Klein, 1990), when members come to know each other's basic theoretical foundations, methodological orientations, and so forth, even if they do not adopt them as their own. At this point in their cognitive development, members are in a position potentially to substitute for each other in discussion, speaking on behalf of another person's perspective at least to a limited extent. They can build on each other's ideas, complement each other's intellectual skills, while becoming aware of their own cognitive limitations (Klein, 1990). This was represented by one of our research team members as follows, "Something happened ... when it actually started to come together.... I could have spoken for other people who were involved in the project. Because now we have kind of this common language, way of describing it that I think is interchangeable."

Common Language

Seeing *through* the lenses of others was another developmental step along the knowledge engagement dimension, implying a richer understanding of disciplinary orientations, and that transformational learning was occurring. Meanings were being restructured and a change in consciousness was emerging (Mezirow, 1991; Mezirow & Associates, 1990). Having common language and shared understanding was now a genuine possibility. We did not have a complete picture of this process, but in some members, we could see it emerging. We also saw the effect, throughout the project, of lack of common language on members' feelings of belonging and satisfaction, as noted by the perspectives shared by three different team members:

> There were additional sources of conflict between the two groups based on language and concept of group process. Superficially, everyone shared a common commitment to "community empowerment," "community participation," "strategic planning," "leadership development," and "needs assessment." However, it rapidly became clear that very different meanings were attached to these ideas.… At root, it became clear that the social development group valued group process and the enhancement of group problem-solving skills as an end in itself, there was somewhat less interest in use of expert models and data development as tools for change. The economic development group, on the other hand, underscored the fact that lack of technical competence and poor goal orientation had sabotaged many well-meaning community improvement efforts.

A second member shared, "The staff lacked a common vision or definition.… It has contributed to divisive and competitive philosophies and demonstrates the lack of trust and commitment." And finally, "Another source of conflict was developing a common language or understanding among ourselves that was meaningful. This also included a meta-language about the philosophy of the project. This is where the greatest conflict occurred for me."

These comments from team members showed how important developing common language can be to group process and interdisciplinary collaboration. They also reflected the struggles in moving to this level of intellectual engagement. Many groups will use the same words in conversation and assume shared meaning, "talking past each other" as Salter and Hearn (1996, p. 148) observe. Disciplinary communities have different ways of speaking about topics, research, methods, and other aspects of academic life. "The same words are used in quite different ways in different disciplines … words are often used as if they have one meaning when different meanings are in fact implied or intended by the various disciplines" (Salter & Hearn, 1996, p. 144). Our research team members often fell into the same trap.

In some respects, this false "shared" understanding let the group move along through early task completion, believing or at least acting as though they were in agreement on the larger issues of the project. It was clear, however, when even small conflicts arose that members were not interpreting words, instructions, activities, and their mission similarly. Without the ability to move beyond parallel understandings to seeing through the lenses of others, many of the interpersonal and intellectual conflicts associated with group work and team development are irreso- lute. Transitioning through these intellectual stages is both a leadership facilitation issue as well as a member cognitive development process. Both take time, especially when members come and go from the team. One member reflected on how member transitions impacted the development of common orientations and language. Part of what was shared was the need for regularly bringing members into the fold. "It is a problem in the sense that anybody new coming in, you have to find ways to bring them so called up to speed. I mean in terms of philosophy and orientation and background ... where they understand what the philosophy and approach is here that's different than what they may be used to." As we saw, after 18 months together, the team was still developing common understandings and language. Yet, they continued to turn in project deliverables and make forward progress in their work.

Several questions come to mind for us in reflecting on the intellectual change processes involved with interdisciplinary collaboration. Is this kind of advanced intellectual development really necessary in faculty work? We would suggest it is a requirement for collaboration as we have defined it. It is especially important in achieving interdisciplinary collabo- ration, by definition. Does common language and shared meaning result in more quality products than more traditional, disciplinary-based approaches to faculty work? We cannot say definitively. It does appear to strongly impact the *process* of faculty work, however. It also greatly impacts the individual learning and development of faculty involved in such pro- cesses. We believe the outcomes and products will look significantly differ- ent. We would like to say that the outcomes from interdisciplinary collaboration efforts are more comprehensive and qualitatively better, but that requires a subjective judgment we are not able to make here.

Cultural Tools as Intellectual Frames

Using sociocultural theories in the examination of interdisciplinary collaboration allows us to focus on the role of cultural tools that enable faculty to communicate with each other and understand their experiences in the world (Lattuca, 2002a; Wertsch, del Rio, & Alvarez, 1995). Although we have discussed the role of disciplinary cultures in reinforcing Stage One behaviors elsewhere in this text, we want also to briefly con- sider cultural tools as intellectual guides for interacting across bound- aries. In our research team, we saw members participating in the intellectual practices of their individual disciplinary cultures as well as in those of the emerging team culture of which they were a part. "Like other cultural tools, disciplines and fields frame the thinking and intellectual activity of individuals who use them.... Discipline refers both to the socio-cultural texts and methods of the discipline and the community of individuals who comprise the disciplinary community of practice" (Lattuca, 2002a, p. 715).

Borrowing or appropriating new cultural tools changes the flow and may alter the entire structure of thought processes (Klein, 1990; Lattuca, 2002a; Wertsch et al., 1995), resulting in new forms of action and thought. From this perspective, multidisciplinarity may be seen as borrowing cultural tools and interdisciplinarity as the internalizing (learning) of these tools in order to study things not well examined with the tools of one's own discipline. We believe the project administrator's original rationale for trying to construct an interdisciplinary team was grounded in this perspective.

Adoption and internalizing transforms individual disciplinary concepts, perspectives, or methods so that they may be used for learning in another field or discipline. As we note in the book's introduction, there are many definitions of interdisciplinarity and borrowing disciplinary tools is only one possible form (Lattuca, 2002b; Salter & Hearn, 1996). Yet, this definition provides a useful example of how mediation and the adoption of intellectual tools from other disciplines can be a transformative act. As a result of internalizing the perspectives of another, we "see" the world in new ways. We are cognitively changed.

We know that the cultural tools of our individual disciplinary orientations have inherent limitations, as much as they have strengths. Our team members were better able to address the complex educational problem proposed to them through an interdisciplinary approach, whereas their individual cultural and intellectual tools left them with traditional (and largely inadequate) responses. They were able to respond to different kinds of questions and issues in ways that were new to them. While we have throughout this text advocated embracing interdisciplinary collaboration as important for higher education, we need to quickly acknowledge that such movement is never without dissonance, qualifiers, and constraints that are literal and figurative. This includes transition along the dimensions we propose in our interdisciplinary collaboration model. Borrowing and adopting the cultural tools from other disciplines may help free faculty from their past disciplinary constraints, but it may also catch them in new ones. In her own study of interdisciplinary work, one of Lattuca's (2002a, p. 726) informants articulated limitations of the intellectual aspects of interdisciplinarity in this way, "One of the reasons why I think interdisciplinarity is always fighting an uphill struggle is because it is not only multi-vocal, it's not only less certain, but it has a softer feel about it. People who have a narrow disciplinary focus are able to say things they think with great confidence. What can interdisciplinary people say with great confidence?"

This concern may exist particularly in the minds of faculty in terms of tenure, promotion, institutional reward structures, and labor market issues that are highly normed on disciplinary traditions more than it speaks to limitations of the concept or utility of interdisciplinarity itself.

SUMMARY

As a result of time spent with and studying our research team, we see interdisciplinary collaboration as a learning process for faculty, leaders, and organizations. This definition causes us then to use different lenses for understanding interdisciplinary collaboration, its impact on individuals and knowledge development, and the way it facilitates collective learning be it within small groups and/or larger organizations. Across all four dimensions of our model including leadership, we find transition to be a function of learning—learning how to integrate disciplinary orientations, learning how to connect to knowledge and knowledge roles differently, learning how to work with others in connected ways, and learning how to facilitate different cognitive development needs of individuals and organizations.

As articulated in many existing learning theories, these transitions require elements of both challenge and support to be accomplished. They include moratoriums, regressions, and breakthroughs, and in all cases, the opportunities for reflection and internalization of new ideas. And as is true in organizational learning literature, a group or collective was involved. The relationships within the group served often as catalysts for the aspects of challenge and support required for learning to occur. In many respects, interdisciplinary collaboration defined as learning processes sets our definition apart from the more casual use of collaboration and cooperation used to describe faculty who work on projects together. And we think the distinctions are critical to understanding the value of interdisciplinary collaboration and its potential impact as a medium for change in the academy.

Critical components of interdisciplinary collaboration viewed from cognitive development perspectives include the need for intellectual neutral space, dialogue, and the development of common language. We saw the importance of all of these to the development of our research team and their work together. Team members grew cognitively as a result of their participation on the team, seeing a broader perspective beyond the confines of their disciplinary boundaries. This is where the new knowledge was created, or at least potential for new knowledge existed as a result of these interactions. However, we were less sure the extent to which the important intellectual components could be orchestrated or predicted by leaders or team members. So, while the process seems clearer to us now, the mechanisms for insuring that process are not always apparent.

CHAPTER 9

CREATING A MOBILE

Leading Interdisciplinary Collaboration

One of the most important issues underlying our research on interdisciplinary collaboration was the role of leaders and leadership. Bennis (1986) has long been concerned that higher education institutions are over managed and under led, and Cronin (1993) suggests that anything that we write about leadership can be refuted. We do not take issue with these authors necessarily, nor the myriad other scholars and writers who fill the shelves of bookstores and libraries with tomes and quick read "how-to" manuals about "leadership." However, we found that writing about leaders and leadership in postsecondary education beyond the presidency remains a less common intellectual exercise than in other private and public sectors, and leadership in interdisciplinary groups, especially as we have defined them, is not well understood. It is also seldom the case that leaders are studied longitudinally, which we were able to do over a period of several months. Whether the leader is formally anointed or appointed by the institution or by the group itself, we felt a critical examination of the leadership supporting (or inhibiting) interdisciplinary collaboration among academics was an important parallel inquiry to the more structural, organizational and intellectual discussions that have come before in this text.

OUR STUDY

Throughout our work with this research team, important issues of leadership emerged. Whether members appreciated the efforts of the project leader, or not, they regularly commented on the importance they felt of having an effective leader and the role of leadership in their collaborative effort. One person went so far as to say, "The single most important element ... in early group process was leadership." In our study, we saw an evolution of leader and leadership that went along with, but did not always directly relate to the changing needs of the team as it developed. The leadership changes emerging from our research team followed the continuum below.

Initially, in Stage One, leadership was directive, bureaucratic, intentional, traditional, and enacted by a single administrator. In accordance with the project leader's senior administrative role within the home institution, she coauthored the original grant, initiated the first call for participation, and was ultimately, administratively accountable for product delivery. This project administrator defined group mission, vision, tasks, and direction at the onset of the project. Team members looked to her for these functions and did not question her authority to enact these roles. They also expected her to serve as conflict negotiator among members and primary communication agent. As the project administrator described her early role, "because [this project] was cross-disciplinary, cross-college and so forth, I took a more assertive role."

In the nature of academic work and the structure of this particular group project, none of the other academics were considered "full-time" on the team, which might account for their initial deference to the project administrator. And in the "Come to Jesus" open call for participation, the starting place for those in attendance was believing their ultimate role was that of "knowledge expert" on an outreach consulting activity. Their lead-

Table 9.1.   Leadership—Interdisciplinary Collaboration Model

	Stage One	*Stage Two*	*Stage Three*
Discipline Orientation	Dominant	Parallel	Integrative
Knowledge Engagement	Expert	Coordinated	Collaborative
Work Orientation	Individual	Group	Team
Leadership Orientation	**Top-Down**	**Facilitative, inclusive**	**Web-like, servant**

ership, per se, was not related to organizational or team processes but if members were leading at all, they saw it as exercising their intellectual expertise. So again, deferring to administrative authority even if outside one's home academic department was not seen as abdicating anything by the team members but more a way of appropriately setting parameters for one's participation. As the project leader indicated, "I saw my role early on as more of a program development role, putting some of the infrastructure in place."

The project administrator hoped for different kinds of faculty involvement during the life of the project, however, and intentionally extended invitations to participate to the broader campus community, She intentionally hoped people from particular departments would become involved because she thought this was the means through which real change might best occur. Believing that complex problems require more complex solutions, the project administrator opted for a multidisciplinary approach to community involvement. Doing so also would potentially change the role of the leader on the project and make a more traditional approach to leadership, at some point, constricting of the innovative processes and intellectual engagement she sought in the team's eventual evolution. How this precisely would play itself out in terms of leadership evolution and this administrator's own connection to the team and project were not clear at the onset. But the lead administrator did seem to have considered that this research project would be a different way of working for all concerned. The project administrator speaks of her initial vision of the project this way, "Professionally, I want the university to have interdisciplinarity. That's complex and has never been done. Personally, I want to have the experience of this. It isn't the first chance I've had for this kind of partnership, but personally, I want to be able to better understand the processes, experience the theories, facilitate leadership, and particularly in [a] community."

At its inception, the team could be best described as leader-oriented. The project leader saw her role as, "Administrative ... developing the team, invitational role [for participation and for ending participation], keeping members focused on developing the program, putting infrastructure in place, identifying resources, steering, instigating the research component so we can reflective about our work.... I was held accountable ... on behalf of the president and the vice provost."

In many ways, her actions in and apart from the group meetings were critical to developing the mechanisms that supported the group's efforts. She was responsible for getting the contracts negotiated and signed, identifying internal and external resources, garnering support from the university, scheduling meetings, and keeping a product timeline on the horizon. She shared, "I would be perceived as a leader because I have fiscal control and probably a final say in many things ... like all kinds of administrative things. So I would be perceived as a leader in terms of administration." Another team member described the project administrator's early role as, "The project leader had extended prior experience ... was sensitive to both rational-technical and affective dimensions of the ... change process, maintained intellectual 'neutrality' in drawing together contrasting perspectives, was able to make decisions and advance the project process in a reasonably timely way, had a clear sense of university mission, and was focused on achieving feasible outcomes within the project period. She was of course not insensitive to political processes within the university."

Although she did not curtail most of the developmental team processes in which she was heavily invested, the project administrator at times needed sometimes to serve as task master, making sure that the typical team storming and forming activities (Tuckman, 1965) did not overshadow evidence of forward movement on the central responsibilities. This was not always a clear balance or an easy leadership task. Often, the project leader used ambiguity as a strategic lever (Weick, 2001), creating a void into which she could insert herself, as negotiator, mediator, and savior. Ambiguity came as ill-defined outcomes, in part because she expected these to emerge from the multidisciplinary lens of the team. Ambiguity also came in the form of paradigmatic negotiations of the team members, and the process of working together in some other form than the traditional knowledge expert/consulting mode common to those involved. It was less the case that the project leader initiated the ambiguous situations than that she chose not to immediately resolve them for the group. This both allowed for team development—dissonance being required before resolution and growth occurs—and increased her own standing within the group when she did "come to the rescue" (Heifetz & Laurie, 1997).

Conflict management skills were required and the ability to create a safe environment for dialogue was important (Bridges & Mitchell, 2000; Senge, 1990, 1996). One member of the research team hinted at the conflict resolution issues present within the team when describing leadership as, "Somebody who can perceive where communication breakdowns are and has the skills to facilitate dialogue that's necessary and resolutions— and identifying potential resolutions."

During Stage Two of the team's development, there was a leadership transition within the team to a person with a more facilitative and inclusive style. This shift was made because of job responsibilities of the project administrator not associated with this project, and although it happened fairly quickly, the decision of a new leader was carefully considered. In the end, the new leader (who we hereafter refer to as the transition leader) was selected from among existing team members. He was a person employed within the same administrative unit as the original project administrator, though his disciplinary orientation to work was similar to that of several team members. In describing his approach, the transition leader expressed,

> I think of myself as being responsible as an enabler in the project. By that, I mean being responsible for trying to see that the different points of view in the project are brought together and issues are identified and that they are resolved. And that's different. I view it as a different kind of leadership ... by that I mean that I think my job is to help bring out the best in everybody else—to establish a structural process where other people can do their best work.

While the approach to leadership changed with the transition leader, final authority for decision making remained with his predecessor because of their different permanent administrative standing within the university. The project administrator characterized the relationship this way: "I think I was a stronger program leader at the beginning and continue to reinforce some of that through [the transition leader]. But I'm hoping [the transition leader] is being perceived as the program leader."

The leadership transition and presence of two individuals who were both considered leaders was not always an ideal situation, when critiqued from a leadership perspective. The move to more enabling leadership was a seemingly appropriate choice as the team continued to evolve to more normative ways of working together, although it did not appear they had quite fully reached this evolutionary status at the time of the leadership change. The combination of a facilitative style used by the transition leader and authority remaining with the more traditional leadership of the project administrator sometimes allowed, or encouraged, team members to stay dependent on the project administrator for conflict resolution and arbitration. One member described the "co"-leadership roles this way: "[The transition leader] has come in and he's filled sort of an administrative complementary role. Unless things get really hot and then you bump it up to [the project administrator]." This is not a criticism of either team leaders, but more a reflection of the preparedness of followers, and their willingness to fully own the team's tasks and responsibility for interpersonal dynamics. It reflected the university's structure that did not allow for a more complete shift of administrative responsibilities and accountabilities to the transition leader. It is also possible that the followers could have been differently prepared for the meaning of the leadership transition, thereby ameliorating some of their continued reliance on the project administrator (Bridges & Mitchell, 2000).

Having remarked about the readiness of followers for leadership changes, it is also important to note that the team was continuing to develop even if all members were not fully on the same plane. Periodically, the group would revert to past, dualistic practices, at which point, members also were more likely to look to the project administrator for traditional leadership. At the same time, shared values were becoming internalized, not merely intellectualized, and often served to guide the development of the team's cognitive lens. The more this occurred, the more these commonly shared values supplanted the need for authoritarian leadership (Cuoto, 2001; DePree, 1998). Leadership could flow more freely through the team members based on the project needs. One member shared this thinking about the role and need of leadership during Stage Two,

> We have to redefine the nature of leadership … and by that I mean we need to evolve from a power based model into an enabling model. We need to evolve from control and management into empowerment, and we need to move from … a linear, "we do this and we do that, and then we do that," bulwark kind of model into a mobile where you have an evolving set of constantly changing set of relationships where you understand and view it in its entirety. We need to move more effectively from power-based relationships into reciprocal relationships.

This comment accurately described the group's transition into a more self-governing and intellectually connected team. Again, while this perspective was not held by all members, its emergence among many was a signal that the team was entering a new phase in its evolution.

As Stage Three emerged, the team had tentatively "normed" (Tuckman, 1965). The leader had to become a skilled convener and work to help members recognize each others' contributions and value to the project overall (Kim & Maubogne, 1993). The team assumed collective leadership responsibility for the work, team maintenance, and development, and so forth. The former authority figure, while still institutionally accountable, shared in the product and process enactment with the rest of the team. As the project administrator shared, "Decisions are made very collaboratively.... It's not the function of my role; it's the maturity of the group." Another member intimated the team's maturation and changed leadership needs this way,

> I think the most effective kind of leadership is sort of where the leader actually follows the lead of the other people. That allows them to have some sort of buy-in process. I mean obviously, there comes a point where if nobody is doing anything you have to step in and say, "Well, would you mind doing this?" but I think the best … approach is, "Ok. Here we are team. What are we going to do? What do you want to do? How do you see that working out?" You know. That's the kind of leadership I think is most effective.

Our research team was indicative of other leadership research examining group formation. When teams are new, occupied with "forming" and "storming" activities (Tuckman, 1965), stronger leadership is often warranted. Members have a greater dependence on the singular, "out front" leader who sees the larger picture and can deal with the cognitive complexities of bringing together multidisciplinary perspectives (Kuhnert & Lewis, 1989). Developing teams establish their own culture, norms, and control mechanisms, and take more responsibility for group processes. The team becomes more internally motivated and self-directed. At this point, the leader must be able to transition from authority to facilitator, guiding the team through task accomplishment and coordinating efforts (Bennis, 1997; Greenleaf, 1996). The leader becoming more facilitative implies ability by other team members to assume leader-like behaviors in the group and to handle the change in a designated leader's role. This shift in leadership, leader style and follower expectations, however, is predicated on the assumption that goals and roles are clear, that trust and effective communication patterns have been established, and that followers see themselves as potential leaders. As the project leader of our research team described,

> One needs to vacillate between being somewhat directive and doing things like consensus building. Especially when there are problems. So [there needs to be] collaborative problem solving, coming to consensus around a common idea, common vision, the direction with a common idea about how we perceive the goal is important.

In the research team we studied, it was not clear that an adoption of collaborative problem solving, common vision, trust and effective communication patterns had all been accomplished at the point at which leader transition occurred, accompanied by a change in style away from more dominant, traditional leadership. The facilitative approach of the new, transition leader at times seemed out of sync with the developmental needs of the team. For example, the approach to conflict resolution between the two leaders was different, and members responded to these styles differently. One member commented,

> When [the project administrator] was involved in the project, she had a tendency to maybe pull somebody aside and make a comment or do something before so I really never saw any of those kinds of comments [tensions]. I'm sure they happened but I never saw them. I think under [the transition leader's] leadership ... the way conflict was resolved was, you know, try to be respectful but maybe some reality checks in terms of boundary maintenance and so on and so forth. I think he appropriately, actively challenged.... One of the ways the group responded to it was by not responding to it. It's like,

"let's get this meeting over with and we'll see you next [time]." Everybody's happy and everybody's rosy but there was always something going on there.

At the same time, members generally responded to the transition leader's facilitation of their processes and he continued to work with the team on its development. One member described, "[The transition leader] is a very easy person to get along with. He has very good people skills. He knows how to frame things in such a way that it's helpful and productive. And he also gives pats on the back when they're well deserved. So he's been a very good leader in that sense."

Even though members appreciated aspects of the transition leader's style, they still reverted to more leader-centered behaviors when there were substantive conflicts. At these times, they looked to the transition leader for firm decision making and strong leadership, even though he was often without the institutional authority or personal inclination needed. Perhaps this is what contributed to periodic questioning by team members of who was really in charge. As another team member explained,

> The strong personalities and charisma of [those] who significantly impacted team activity and the University reporting structures in which team leaders were located also confounded leadership efforts. Authority, power, and final decision making responsibility rested in different places, depending on the issue. For example, because of [the project administrator's] university position, certain functional aspects of team activity (e.g., budget approval and contract negotiation) remained vested in the original leader even after she stepped back from the project and a new leader assumed responsibility for the team's daily activities. While this did not necessarily hamper progress toward goal achievement for the team, it did result in some leadership role confusion at times for most members of the team.

LEADERSHIP CHALLENGES

Several challenges became clear during the course of our research that confronted the project administrator and transition leader. These challenges impacted leadership ability, focused leadership energy at times, and provided opportunities for the leaders to facilitate the growth of team members in interesting ways. These challenges also seemed to require reflective thinking and cognitive growth on the part of the leaders, themselves. We focus this discussion on several leadership challenges: institutional challenges, the concept of team leadership, the role of cultural leadership, and membership issues that confronted the team and the leaders.

Institutional Challenges

There were significant institutional challenges associated with the project we studied that might occur in any interdisciplinary collaboration effort. For example, administrative processes will likely never be reconfigured fully to the disparate needs of interdisciplinary group efforts, matrix organizations, or other creative units addressing complex problems. As a result, any such activity exists within extant organizational structures and cultures, at least to some extent.

Bringing together the right persons who are in control of the right processes at the right time and creating a management structure that best supports the team efforts is a leadership challenge needing careful planning and time for design, agreement, and negotiation. Most funded projects do not allow for this kind of time after the award is made, and it is difficult to anticipate all the pitfalls and concerns in advance of an actual contract award. It is clear in this study that a leader who understands the institution's management workings, and who has effective administrative and negotiating skills is an important principal player. Obviously, these same talents also aid the leader in effectively dealing with structural inhibitors.

Many of the structural, institutional inhibitors had organizationally political overtones (Morgan, 1999; Scott, 2002). Power, resource allocation, ownership, and coalition building were political aspects of the interdisciplinary collaboration project common to many academic activities, and ones that required a certain kind of leader to mediate. In the case of our research team, Stage One team development was characterized by incidences of political wrangling including contract and budget negotiation, attempts by team members to exert disciplinary biases over the project definitions and strategies, interpersonal struggles for control, and testing of team norms and boundaries. These examples were fairly typical of any early team development struggles (Bolman & Deal, 1997; Morgan, 1999) and required a leader who was politically savvy, an effective negotiator, and one who was not strongly aligned with political hot buttons (e.g., one disciplinary paradigm or another, individual team members).

Team Leadership

As noted, the multidisciplinary nature of the team brought its own set of human resource issues (Bolman & Deal, 1997; Morgan, 1999; Scott, 2002). Team development and interdisciplinary collaboration are time-consuming experiments where process is as important as product. Disciplinary distinctions need to be addressed; identity issues of knowledge expert, independent researcher, and entrepreneurial technical assistant have to be reconciled; and relationship and behavioral norms established. Additionally, because of the cross-departmental nature of the team, internal monitoring mechanisms needed to be established since the team was less able to utilize those of the large university, such as traditional disciplinary or departmentally-based reward structures and ways of sanctioning/curtailing inappropriate behavior.

Actively socializing people to the team, keeping them involved and their work interconnected, and dealing effectively with the varying range and style of interpersonal interaction are process factors that, in the end, affect any kind of collective work. In addition, leaders have to understand the interpersonal side of team development, especially when disciplinary boundaries need to be crossed. All of this requires attention, regular communication, and on-going maintenance (Bensimon & Neumann, 1993; Bolman & Deal, 1999). As the project leader described,

> I think leadership is critical, I really do. To convince as many people that this is what we are about, this is what we are to do. Trying to push people to see, to create a whole, to understand the whole, and live within the whole. I think it is time to push people to see, to understand their role, and to have a common vision. It goes beyond common vision. Yes, we are all involved with this, but it needs a common implementation of the vision.

In some respects, these examples may be fairly common of any early team development struggles and yet, especially in contractual situations like funded research, sufficient time to develop the normative and cultural infrastructure to support team functioning is often minimized if not eliminated altogether. Conflict resolution and shared decision making become less common than burying conflict and orchestrating decision making apart from the group (Scott, 2002). These group issues are also expected when we consider academic teams from a human resources perspective (Bolman & Deal, 1997; Morgan, 1999), and yet, faculty (and academic administrators) often intellectualize their work, focusing on the "science" of research rather than the interpersonal aspects of it. While faculty acknowledge the human relationship inherent in classroom teaching, they seem less willing to see the positive and negative effects of relationships also present in collective work beyond instruction. Leaders and team members need to better grasp these interpersonal dynamics, especially when crossing the "safe havens" of disciplinary strongholds. Team maintenance activities that support effective processes need to be as much a focus as product delivery for all concerned.

Leadership authors from across the disciplines such as Senge (1990; 1996), Helgeson (1995), Heider (1989), Bennis (1997), Tierney (1991, 1999) and many others, argue leadership should be disseminated throughout the organization, and not just kept within the purview of one or two designated leaders. This is another aspect of team leadership that was part of our interdisciplinary collaboration model. As we watched the cognitive development of our research team from a set of individual knowledge experts to a more intellectually integrated team, we saw and heard the leadership needs change. They evolved, as noted in the model from top-down and hierarchical, to web-like and servant. This transition is not a function of time alone. Nor is it something that can be fully orchestrated or controlled. But there are ways in which leaders can facilitate the requisite learning of members so that team leadership takes hold.

Role of Cultural Leadership

Patterns of behavior and shared meanings given to actions and words are important components of organizational life. They distinguish members from nonmembers, ameliorate ambiguity, offer a sense of connection and intrinsic reward, and provide a sense of belonging and purpose that can carry a group through difficult times. They are also organizational aspects that require effort to cultivate and support, since meaning has to be ascribed to them and made conscious in the minds of members (Bolman & Deal, 1997; Bugay, 2001; Masland, 1985). In the same way that a team is not a team because it has been labeled as such, a cultural artifact is not an aspect of normative glue just because the leader says so. But a leader can be very instrumental in shaping culture and to fostering its growth.

Leadership is entwined with culture formation (Schein, 1985). A leader using a cultural approach to interdisciplinary collaboration and team development looks for ways to reinforce stories and myths, to use jargon and create shared language, to celebrate achievements and ritualize activities so that members regularly feel a sense of connection to a greater whole (Bolman & Deal, 1997; Tierney, 1991). As an example, socialization of new members takes on greater significance from a cultural perspective. It becomes an intentional process of reinforcing the norms and values, an opportunity to clarify mission, roles and goals, and celebrate team accomplishments, rather than a coincidental, informal happening.

In the research team we studied, although it was not used very often or particularly cultivated as a leadership strategy, organizational culture was an important consideration in team development. Therefore, cultural leadership could be quite useful to leaders who want to be very active in shaping culture and to fostering its growth (Kanter, 1999). When it occurred, effective cultural leadership led to great strides in team development. Using celebrations as vehicles for reinforcing group goals, trying to develop common language, and leaving situations unresolved for strategic periods of time to build creative tension and interdependence within the group were examples of cultural leadership the project administrator used to the group's advantage. What was also clear was that there were many missed opportunities for providing the organizational theatre to strengthen team functioning (Bolman & Deal, 1997; Morgan, 1999) and enhance overall team development through cultural leadership.

We believe leaders must pay attention simultaneously to the three dimensions of growth and development (discipline orientation, knowledge engagement, and work orientation) identified in the interdisciplinary collaboration model. These dimensions affect each other and may require different approaches to leadership and development over time, including the use of cultural leadership. The team's development must be purposeful and nurtured along these continua, and leaders need to bridge intellectual boundaries with the skills of an idea integrator, rapporteur, and fundraiser.

Even with effective leadership, there was a need to arrive at a politically neutral construct for community engagement that all members of the team could accept. In facilitating team development along the dimensions of the interdisciplinary collaboration model, it seemed necessary to find a neutral intellectual space that afforded all parties a way of moving forward from dominant to parallel knowledge engagement without losing face. This intellectual neutral space took a long time to emerge for our research team yet, was necessary for the their transition from Stage One to Stage Two. Being aware of the potential need for and knowing how to interject or create the neutral construct or space seems a valuable leadership lesson learned from this study.

Some questions we were left with, then, include can a single person effectively lead a group through the stages of interdisciplinary team development? If so, how does one develop this set of skills and understandings beyond the "simplistic" notions of contingency or situational leadership? And finally, how is this leader sustained through her own cognitive transitions as she tries to facilitate interdisciplinary collaboration team development?

Membership Issues

As is true with any extended group effort, including faculty academic work, the "length of stay" of each member is dictated by numerous circumstances. In the academy, teaching loads, contract dates, advising responsibilities, committee assignments, administrative tasks, and other research all converge on any single activity in which a faculty member may choose to get involved. The lengthy nature of collaborative work, as noted in earlier chapters, can be particularly challenging because it likely crosses multiple boundaries of time, space, budget, and department. As a result, when initiating an 18-month funded collaborative research activity, one should expect team member turnover and all the sundry consequences of such changes. We found the expectation to be true for our research team and the consequences, while perhaps anticipated, not always easy to address. Regular team maintenance, socialization processes when new persons joined the team, establishing and re-establishing communication patterns, and mutual understandings of roles and role expectations were just a few issues articulated by members of the group as they commented on the effect of membership transitions. Member transitions affect everyone on the team, but should be of particular concern to the leader.

One member captured some of the negative and positive aspects of membership that confronted this team:

> It's such a natural ongoing component of any group process that one can cite positive things when people have left the team and negative things when people have left the team. It is a loss or a dream. So I think the group as a whole has to assimilate these changes. Obviously, I am still expressing the loss of [one member] as kind of a coleader of the project. I think about how much time we lose.... How much time we've invested in two other individuals. So it is time consuming and the group feels that you have to reorient, re-enculture to the group. But it is not necessarily always a negative thing, so ... I believe these are part of group work, some kind of growing. I think you have a critical mass for a long enough period of time, so that they have a sense of a group.

Other team members also expressed mixed emotions about the changes that took place in the team over the life of the project.

> Interestingly enough, I'm pleased that the team goes on as part of the tangents and that it is by and large, individuals who have been able to come and go and the process goes on. I mean we shifted project directors, local project directors, and the process went on, not without a hitch completely, but it went on relatively smoothly given the size of the change. People have come in and then left ... as old people have left and new people have come in, we've had a new blood in the sense of new ideas and fresh viewpoints and people becoming active who really never intended to be part of the team.

And another shared, "My curiosity is with people who have fallen away from the project, whether it was a matter of honesty with each other and that continuing commitment, probably."

The transition leader spoke specifically to some of the responsibilities associated with member transition when he shared,

> [One group that was participating] really have not been part of the team and should be and I think that's partly having to do with time and conflicts, but I see that problem and I see that as my problem to resolve. One of the things I should have done and planned to do in my enabling role is to draw them in as regular team members and we paid the price for some of that in still unresolved conflicts.

Some team members concurred with the transition leader's not having met his objectives to integrate new members to the team. One person's views captured some of the frustration felt by some team members: "If there really is a team, why don't we even handle these changes [in membership] as a team? And why don't we talk about the next year's project as a team? You know the people at the top that pull the strings and then those of us who implement what they tell is us is to be done.... I guess we are between the devil and the deep blue sea."

In the end, if member transition is not handled effectively by the leader and/or by other team members, it can have negative effects on the processes of the group and on the intellectual synergy. Unstable team membership leads to unwillingness to take risks and a commitment to the lone-scholar/expert work orientation (Klein, 1990) common in Stage One of our interdisciplinary collaboration model. Somehow, additions to the team need to be socialized and acculturated into the workings of the team—its objectives and goals, its values and operating principles, and its personality. The consequences of not attending to this team maintenance function can be great to both those who are not appropriately socialized and to others who have remained with the team. In thinking about those who came "late" to the project team, one member stated, "[Change in team membership] has affected the team in that members were put on and didn't even know why they were on the team. They didn't know the mission. So you don't know the mission, then you don't know the grounds of engagement."

Another member reflected on how changes in the team affected his sense of his own role on the team:

> [Change in team membership] initially in terms of group cohesion, it really sort of blew any shot at that and we were sort of like, we were all sort of waiting around wondering who was going to drop out next and like, "do I really want to be here" kind of thing. We were the "sole survivors" and we had "done it" and so therefore, there was a great deal of camaraderie, a great collective sense of accomplishment. In that regard, there was a lot of cohesion.

When members leave, especially in a team that has moved through the dimensions of Stage One of our interdisciplinary collaboration model into Stages Two or Three, more than a skill set has been lost. A real piece of the puzzle, a way of thinking, a contributor to the overall intellectual work and philosophic ethos of the team has also been lost. And may not be easily replaced. As one member recounted, "There were a number of project stage changes within the first six months.... It is difficult to build a body of cumulative organizational experience and faculty expertise under these circumstances."

It is certainly not realistic to assume that every group involved with interdisciplinary collaboration will remain intact throughout its life span. But we observed some leadership and member challenges associated with transition on this kind of team that are of note to prospective leaders, and that require conscious attention if the collaboration is to thrive.

LEADING AND LEARNING

As we realized in studying our research team, leading interdisciplinary collaboration efforts is about facilitating learning for the members of the group and for the leader. Vaill (1997, p. 4) calls this orientation the "learning premise" and suggests that being involved in a learning process or proceeding from a learning premise means to be, "continually confronted with newness—new problems, ideas, techniques, concepts; new gestalts; new possibilities and new limits; new awareness and understandings of oneself. Learning also means reinterpreting things already understood letting go of former understandings and techniques, even if at the level of brain physiology one never literally 'unlearns.'"

Thinking about the leadership we saw in this regard changes the focus away from administration and management skill acquisition, and really reflects the transitions across the interdisciplinary collaboration dimensions that emerged. It allows us to broaden the definition of leadership and, by conceptualizing leadership as learning, we relinquish the need for a specific career orientation and can look at the ways in which leadership is developed and shared throughout the organization. We arrive, then, at a specific point of discussion: leading cognitive team development.

In a collective where both technical and intellectual skills are involved, leaders have to focus on helping faculty become active inquirers into their own and others' practices. Bartlett (1990) spoke to the same thing we portrayed in our discussion of the intellectual aspects of interdisciplinary collaboration when she wrote, "Because knowledge arises within social contexts and in multiple forms, the key to increasing knowledge lies in an effort to extend one's limited perspective" (p. 882); to learn. Members need to recognize that their expertise is "special knowledge, but limited knowledge" and that they need to move beyond their own knowledge spheres, "to understand other perspectives" (p. 882). This is done, in part, by acquiring new lenses for critically assessing team circumstances and members' role (including the leader) in determining these circumstances (Smyth, 1989, p. 190).

Throughout Stage One and beyond, our research team struggled in moving beyond their expert knowledge, reflected in many competing definitions of "right strategies" subconsciously defined by their disciplinary orientations (Senge, 1998). The traditional expert thinking characteristic of faculty training reinforced the need to express a right answer in order to prove one's intellectual standing in the group. With the leader's help, team members needed to move toward strategic thinking, which required transitions in their work orientation and knowledge engagement (moving into Stage Two). Strategic thinking reaps richer rewards, but it is more difficult to implement than reliance on "right strategy" thinking. Senge argues that achieving insight into the nature of the complexity and formulating concepts and world views for coping with it (strategic thinking) are more important than the quick fixes of singular strategies. He is less clear on exactly how to accomplish this. After 18 months of team development processes, our members had no fail-safe strategies, either.

The project administrator characterized the leadership needs of the team as, "strong intellectual leadership." We agree and see this as a primary leadership challenge of working with interdisciplinary collaboration. Rather than simply doling out tasks, leaders cultivate an enabling capacity or empowering environment that stimulates faculty to frame problems rather than waiting for the leader(s) to do so. Leaders give the work back to members (Heifetz & Laurie, 1997). In so doing, members are helped to discuss and work individually and collectively at understanding and changing the situations that caused these problems. As one member of our research team shared, "I'm understanding the way we approach research and collaborative research. I think there are lessons." Helping members to see this as a primary function of their collective objectives is a very different orientation to faculty work than we sometimes see, and a different academic leadership function. Not that product delivery is unimportant, but the cognitive enterprise *is* important.

This kind of individual and collective development is more challenging for team members and for leaders than work framed in the expert paradigm of Stage One. It takes longer, develops more slowly, is cultivated through dialogue rather than delegation, and challenges core beliefs of members. It is rarely easy, often exciting, and demands capable leaders fully aware of the need for challenge and support as intellectual development occurs. Effective facilitators may be those best able to serve as cognitive leaders, yet when pulling together faculty for group work, we often continue to rely on traditional variables such as rank and professional expertise for selecting group leaders. Leaders chosen primarily for these reasons may fall subject to the same kinds of Stage One thinking as group members originally experienced, relying on expertise and authority to wield power and influence. This is ineffective in leading cognitive development and the shift to a different leadership philosophy may cause inherent dissonance for the leader.

Perhaps there are other leader understandings to consider. Astin and Astin (2000, p. 12) suggest that, "the most effective group leadership effort is the one that can serve as a collaborative learning environment for its members," and we certainly would agree based on the evolution of the research team we studied. We found that the leader, also, has to have a personal learning strategy (Heifetz & Laurie, 1998) in order to facilitate learning in others.

One team member echoed the facilitation needs and thought about the cognitive team changes as he related to leadership this way:

> During the early months, I was impressed by the extent to which the project leader was able to guide the group toward a relatively balanced infusion of perspectives from both sides. To some extent, of course, I have created a false dichotomy here. There were in fact bridges and motivators that allowed people to make intellectual connections. For example … all were in fact interested in ensuring that people … would be meaningfully engaged— all felt a sense of hope and potentiality in the project—and with good group facilitation by the project leader, all were able to articulate viewpoints without too much denigration of those not in agreement.

The leadership of the project administrator described above has little to do with hierarchical position and expert authority. It has everything to do with enabling the best ideas to emerge from wherever they come, through a process of informed and rational dialogue. Even though it was clear in our study that this facilitating dialogue was key to transition along the interdisciplinary collaboration continuum, the entire orientation to leadership is a significant challenge when the larger organizational focus remains on efficiency and accountability. Smyth (1989) and others argue that this particular organizational focus, so common in the academy, prevents faculty from situating their pedagogical processes within the broader social and cultural categories of education (p. 192). Therefore, real intellectual change and paradigm shifts, including interdisciplinarity, are less possible.

Cognitive development of team members does not always yield a learning organization, but a learning organization does require the cognitive development of team members so looking more closely for a moment at this concept seems appropriate. Senge (1998) says that leadership in learning organizations is subtler and ultimately more important work than in the traditional view of leaders. Although we certainly believe that leadership was important throughout the life of the research team we studied, Senge's perspective seems particularly borne out in the evolution of this team and the perspectives of its members. They transitioned in their leader expectations from top-down, out-front more traditional leader behavior to more of a feeling of collective responsibility. There were still expectations for the project administrator, but typically more in times of serious conflict or when the team bumped up against institutional bureaucracies and politics. One could argue that, rather than a leader per se, the team sometimes needed an effective manager who could handle organizational processes. The project administrator seemed aware of this when she said, "It's been my experience that if you keep the administration out of it, others, particularly faculty, can do what they do best." Her efforts to deflect as much of the administrivia as possible from the team perhaps illustrates this philosophy of practice. Her approach seemed to pave the way for continued focus on intellectual development while she was the leader and also for the transition leader.

The transition leader of the team reflected on the status of the group's learning almost 18 months into the project. He shared, "We need to get better at dealing with one another within the team.... I think some of the new areas of cooperative learning, learning in group process or understanding of how groups learn, how people function in groups and groups as a way of transferring knowledge and information. I think we can do a lot better in that area." It was clear in his comments that he defined his role and the team's achievements in part around the ideas of individual and group cognitive development. Leading the team was, for him, facilitating the intellectual growth of its members in order to reach the desired results emanating from interdisciplinary collaboration.

SUMMARY

One of the most important issues underlying our research on interdisciplinary collaboration was the role of leaders and leadership. Throughout our work with this research team, we saw leaders and leadership evolve, but in ways that did not always directly relate to the changing needs of the team. The leader role began as top-down, directive, and more traditional, and the team could best be described as leader-centered. It was the project administrator's grand scheme and she set the early stages of participation. A leadership change during Stage Two saw a transition leader designated from among existing team members whose style was more facilitative than administrative. As the team continued to develop, members assumed more collective responsibility for group maintenance, decision making, norms, and dialogue.

Although in our research team, the leader transition that resulted in a different leadership style may not have come exactly on par with the team's development, we conclude that there needs to be continued assessment of the leadership needs of the team and appropriate adjustments made by the leader. This implies leaders have the cognitive ability to effectively determine team needs and to be able to actually adjust their own style from authoritarian to servant-like. We recognize this may not be cognitively possible for every leader of every group, including an interdisciplinary collaboration, but the transition does seem to best serve the needs of the team.

There were several leadership challenges throughout the project. Of particular note in the discussion of interdisciplinary collaboration is membership continuity, culture development including fostering common language, and facilitating member growth across discipline orientation, knowledge engagement, and work orientation simultaneously. This clearly represented leadership with a particular emphasis on individual and group learning, in addition to any more formal product delivery. More contemporary descriptors of leaders capture the essence of this mode of leading, including phrases such as boundary agent, midwife, and steward. Cultivating member cognitive development is an important aspect of leadership in interdisciplinary collaborations, and requires of the leader the capacity to see things themselves from multiple perspectives. These leaders need to be cognitively complex thinkers, who have skills in critical thinking, listening, and knowing how to learn. Whether we call it a learning organization, a cognitive team, or in our case, an interdisciplinary collaboration, bringing together integrated thinkers across multiple perspectives requires higher order leadership skills than reflected in traditional, hierarchical group work. It need not be embodied in the person with the title or the appointed "leader", but without this form of leadership present throughout the group's tenure, we believe there will not be transitions along the interdisciplinary collaboration model we propose.

CHAPTER 10

CONCLUSION

In this concluding chapter, we want to step back from the research in which we were involved and think more broadly about the concept of interdisciplinary collaboration as a form of academic work. We consider some of the cross-cutting themes that emerged from our model and the frame discussions that constituted the earlier chapters of this text. It is also important to think about this work in new ways. Where does the study of interdisciplinary collaboration leave us and, more importantly, where does it take us in the academy? If our understandings have merit, how can they inform others and perhaps improve the discourse around organizational learning and change?

We focus our attention in several areas. Studying faculty is typically a multifaceted proposition, or should be, so the ways in which interdisciplinary collaboration as a form of faculty work is facilitated or inhibited require consideration from many angles. In the end, we want to emphasize the ideas of neutrality, rethinking academic work, and leading the learning organization.

NEUTRALITY

Perhaps the most important concept providing foundation for our model is the concept of neutrality. Without it, the power and politics of the academy surely sabotage any interdisciplinary experiment. In this book, we have talked about both organizational and intellectual neutral space. We

---

Breaking Out of the Box: Interdisciplinary Collaboration and Faculty Work, 131–146

believe these two concepts are each important if a faculty group is to move from disciplinary experts to integrative thinkers, from working as individuals to working as an interdisciplinary team. An apolitical or neutral environment is necessary to support integrative thinking.

The Neutral Self

While we have been direct in our beliefs about the intellectual and structural neutral space, we have only implied that each member of the interdisciplinary collaboration also needs to reach a neutral self, one where disciplinary presumptions about the world are suspended, where egos are left at the door, and where openness to new perspectives and learning can take place. Faculty must be able to find that intellectual neutral space, and before they can find it, they must be able to become neutral themselves.

Some faculty seem more predisposed in their ability to seek a neutral self than others. This was certainly true on our research team, and has been noted in the work of others studying this topic (Klein, 1990; Lattuca, 2002a; Salter & Hearn, 1996). Klein (1990, p. 183) articulates some common traits of faculty predisposed to interdisciplinary work, noting they are often reliable, flexible, patient, resilient, sensitive to others, risk taking, have a thick skin, and a preference for diversity and new social roles. We would add the attributes of being open minded, an active listener, self-reflective, and excited about intellectual engagement. Klein uses several labels for faculty/researchers inclined toward interdisciplinary collaboration including adventurers, divergent thinkers, analogic thinkers, boundary spanners, and academic intellectuals. These labels bring to mind different images of faculty than those we would use to stereotype Stage One thinkers. Successful interdisciplinary collaborators are willing to shed their disciplinary shackles, at least periodically, and put on the perspectives of others. Those who are able to place themselves outside of the bounds of disciplinary dogma are most able to achieve neutral self. Suspending disciplinary biases and moving to neutral self provides the cognitive basis for intellectual neutral space. Members are able to dialogue and develop common language, and can move to Stage Two and Stage Three behaviors and thinking.

The Neutral Structure

From a structural perspective, how do universities create the environment of neutrality that fosters interdisciplinary collaboration efforts? We argue this process begins with an organizationally neutral space. One version of this is a matrix organization without specific disciplinary association, located in the provost office, graduate school office, an independent structure, or an externally funded (also neutral) office. The office in which the matrix is located can perform the administrivia required to manage the bureaucratic resources necessary to support the interdisciplinary collaboration. In addition, this office might provide the project leader for the temporary matrix. This largely characterizes the research team we studied. Organizationally located in and structurally supported through a university outreach office, the project administrator also was a senior leader in that unit.

Other organizationally neutral structures could include cross-disciplinary research institutes (Klein, 1990) and soft project units to which faculty from different academic areas may be assigned or affiliate themselves for defined project work (Tierney, 1999). In these alternate structures, it remains important that the leader be seen as organizationally neutral so that disciplinary and departmental power games do not bias the project or preclude (or dictate) faculty participation. Without removing as much of these dominating structures and cultures as possible, even if they all do not evaporate, the learning of interdisciplinary collaboration is curtailed and Stage One thinking and behaviors are reinforced. Organizational neutral space becomes a kind of prerequisite for developing intellectual neutral space, or at least a conduit to this kind of cognitive engagement.

The Neutral Leader

Even in the organizationally neutral structures described above that may ameliorate power and political advantages among disciplinary participants, it is equally important that the project leader be seen as organizationally neutral. Disciplinary and departmental politics less easily bias the project and affect faculty participation because they are not believed to be advocated by a leader who is perceived to be organizationally neutral. In addition, project leaders must have an intellectual openness themselves and adhere to the same cognitive neutrality as group members in order to set an example and facilitate development of Stage Two and Stage Three thinking.

We recognize the leadership difficulty in fostering intellectual neutral space, and saw the challenges first hand in our research team. The leader has to set a neutral tone through their own behaviors, the way they facilitate discussion and debate, the openness they show in their own reaction to new ideas, and so forth. They have to create a safe environment in conjunction with other team members so that paradigm exploration can take place, especially during the more cognitively volatile periods of Stage One and early Stage Two, even though they can not *make* members do this intellectual work. Leaders have to encourage the often time consuming and emotionally challenging work of developing intellectual neutral selves among team members while simultaneously meeting project deadlines and expectations for deliverables.

Given that many faculty will not be able to shed or suspend their disciplinary reins, or interested in doing so, we recognize that not every group will be successful at achieving interdisciplinary thinking. Each member must be a boundary spanner, a divergent thinker able to acquire a neutral self, and help in creating a neutral intellectual space with the group. The leaders needs to establish the safe haven for creative thinking, listening, and effective interpersonal dynamics early in the group's formation. This requires skills in personnel management, conflict resolution, goal and role clarification, and so forth, typical of administrators in any organization. It also requires a management of self (Bennis, 1986) including awareness of one's own disciplinary biases, mental models about academic work, an ability to learn across spheres of knowledge, and exercise intellectual openness or neutrality. We can not overemphasize the importance of leader neutrality in determining the success of interdisciplinary collaboration. The leadership challenge in facilitating interdisciplinary collaboration is significant; we remain convinced it is important.

VALUING INTERDISCIPLINARY COLLABORATION

One of the primary goals of this study was to understand how, and if, academics would come together to work across disciplines. We wanted to know what academic work would look like if interdisciplinary collaboration was really embraced by the participants and the departments in which they worked. What we found in this research on interdisciplinary collaboration are a number of factors that affected ability of faculty to move beyond the boundaries of their role, their definitions of work, and the institutional expectations held for them as academics. In our discussion of organizational structures and cultures, we raised a number of issues that inhibited interdisciplinary collaboration and some ways in which those specific issues may be addressed to facilitate more easily this important learning process. We also have long considered the risks in discussing these inhibitors and facilitators as discrete or separate ideas, fearing that we reinforce the piecemeal and first-order change processes so common in postsecondary education.

We debated extensively how we could talk about changing academic work to incorporate interdisciplinary collaboration without talking about values, and decided it is impossible. All that we do in the academy begins with what we value. Research universities value knowledge creation, and reward it. And while teaching and service, or outreach, are important values held by academe, knowledge creation is the currency that drives the research institution (Bronstein & Ramaley, 2002; Fairweather, 1996; Tierney, 1999). Look at any research university; look at any discipline; see what activity is most richly rewarded and you will see what is most valued. Rewards are incentives to do those things the organization values. What is valued and what is rewarded in a research university is Stage One behavior. We promote the disciplinary expert who works individually, publishes individually, and contributes to the disciplinary field by expanding the knowledge base within the often rigid and accepted boundaries of the discipline. As our model suggests, these values run counter to the espoused values and behaviors of interdisciplinary collaboration.

Creating interdisciplinary solutions to complex societal problems should be recognized, valued, and rewarded as richly as theory building. Those outside higher education might even argue that solving complex societal problems from an interdisciplinary perspective should be valued more highly as it may have more impact on the quality of life outside the university. It is not out intent to decide this debate but to claim that both activities should be valued within the university reward structure. Yet, we are still left to question how does a research institution, which claims to value knowledge creation, change or expand the value system and disciplinary and institutional cultures to encourage and reward interdisciplinary behavior when it seriously contradicts the traditional model of faculty work?

This is a difficult question to answer. Using our own model as a point of departure, we could say that a typical administrative approach to incorporating interdisciplinary collaboration would be to focus on elements of this kind of work that fit the existing system; if there is dissonance, identify the problem and fix it within the culture and climate as they presently exist. This "single-loop" analysis (Argyris & Schon, 1977; Senge, 1990) looks at interdisciplinary collaboration as a means of faculty activity that works as long as it fits. We can look at traditional definitions of collaboration and see this approach in action, since the goal is mending problems to maintain the status quo work life. For example, academic rhetoric is far more inclined post-Boyer (1990) to value "collaborative" publications ... as long as author contribution can still be clearly identified and field-specific outlets are used for dissemination (Foster-Fishman & Stevens, 2002), unless the faculty member does not really want to "count" the work. Most faculty do not question the values of the evaluation and reward structure and whether they can be expanded to also value interdisciplinary collaboration as we have defined it. Rather, faculty typically settle for cooperative work that fits more easily into the existing norms. We also recognize that the university is faced with a serious dilemma if it truly wants to review or assess the value of interdisciplinary activity. Sole authorship versus coauthored publications, the quality and acceptance of the publication outlet (disciplinary versus interdisciplinary), the life of the review cycle, the peer group for review, and assessment all present problems for which we admittedly have few answers.

At the same time, in moving the conversation forward, we think it is largely counterproductive to frame support of interdisciplinary collaboration as an either-or dichotomy. Changing disciplinary cultures is an extremely challenging task and we do not advocate overthrowing them since disciplines are the knowledge bases from which interdisciplinarity comes. Nor are we suggesting replacing disciplinarity with interdisciplinarity. Still, some change in the value system is necessary to nurture and support interdisciplinary collaboration and this avenue of knowledge creation.

We believe interdisciplinary collaboration is better served if we try to expand the disciplinary and academic cultural systems to incorporate the values of interdisciplinarity, an extension of the values of the traditional expert model. Creation of interdisciplinarity or integrative knowledge should be rewarded equitably with creation of disciplinary knowledge. Collaboration as we define it in the introduction to this book should be recognized and rewarded as richly as individual accomplishments. We need to encourage the time for reflection that permits exploring the cognitive dissonances one experiences when fundamental beliefs are made conscious and challenged in dialogue with others instead of encouraging premature closure that better fits the traditional work patterns. The time it takes to explore paradigms and create interdisciplinary collaboration and integrative thinking should be valued and acknowledged by university administrators and faculty review committees as much as work conducted through the application of singular expert knowledge.

If we really want to create change and reform in academic work, therefore, we need to fundamentally question the models used to evaluate and reward faculty (Argyris & Schon; 1976; Senge, 1990). We need to construct different approaches to discipline and department cultural constructions that allow intellectual innovation, including interdisciplinary collaboration, to be a norm rather than the difficult exception. This presents a much more significant and sometimes threatening set of challenges, and certainly a form of deep change we are not often accustomed to in the fast paced, "do more with less" consumer higher education environment of today. But we recall the sentiments of one of our team members when he thought about the 18-month project in which he had been involved. His comments were not reflective of first-order change and quick fixes. Rather, he spoke eloquently about the transformational change he saw the group experiencing:

> I see a massive accomplishment (for the time spent) really. We really only have been working on this for a year and one half. Given the task at hand, I think that's [group growth] extraordinary because we are dealing with actual fundamental values and beliefs of all of us that have had to change, myself included. We're dealing with a complex multilevel system change ... that is, psychological levels, sociological levels, interpersonal levels, personality issues, economic issues, historical issues. It's like an onion with a thousand layers.

CHANGING ACADEMIC WORK TO ACCOMMODATE INTERDISCIPLINARY COLLABORATION

As noted, we do not want to raze the present university system and discard decades and decades of traditional knowledge engagement. But we do want to find ways of including this integrative form of knowledge engagement more equitably so that faculty who choose to get involved can find it professionally rewarding to do so. One important consideration in altering forms and beliefs about academic work is recognizing the difference between administrative priorities and their adoption by faculty (Austin & Moore, 1997). When academic administrators want to emphasize interdisciplinary collaboration in the reward structure, for example, they often find it does not lead necessarily to this work being integrated and linked to the rest of faculty activities. For initiatives to become more readily accepted as part of the culture and values, we need to rethink the nature of academic work, redefine aspects of the mission (e.g., outreach), rebalance or realign attention and commitment, and reinvent or integrate across the mission (Austin & Moore, 1997).

We saw evidence of these same change elements occurring, or needing to occur for members of our research team and their home unit administrators and peers. We saw how challenging it was for some members of our research team to integrate the interdisciplinary collaboration activity into the rest of their academic responsibilities, especially if they did not have strong departmental support for this work. Initiatives that support interdisciplinary collaboration often motivate only those who already are involved because the work is initially viewed as out of the norm. This is quite similar to the way that instructional development programs to enhance teaching lie on the periphery of "mainstream faculty work" and therefore, typically affect only those with the greatest a priori investment. If interdisciplinary collaboration and other forms of innovative academic work were seen as part of a department's, college's, or institution's collective agenda, and so seen as a valuable contribution, it may make faculty participation easier. It should also make the individual member efforts at interdisciplinary collaboration feed more readily back into departmental accountability and accomplishments.

Faculty roles have grown increasingly complex in research universities, as well as other postsecondary institutions, but these responsibilities have been added with little reshaping of the surrounding environment, with little reorienting of institutional reward structures, or with little examination of the interrelated components of the institutional structure in which the work takes place (Colbeck, 1998). We have not stopped to ask "should we?" and "how does this really make a difference?" as often as we have just accepted the increased work, albeit begrudgingly. So when we talk about finding ways to support interdisciplinary collaboration as a form of faculty work, we want not to fall into the same trap. We have asked ourselves whether or not faculty should be involved in interdisciplinary collaboration and whether or not it really makes a difference, and have found affirming answers to both questions.

What we find ourselves asking with less clear responses is how do we enhance, expand, or recreate organizational and disciplinary cultures to support interdisciplinary collaboration while still affirming the tradition of the discipline? Most interdisciplinary collaborations are temporary and shorter term within the faculty career. After the problem at the epicenter of work has been resolved, the interdisciplinary collaboration usually disbands. Faculty return to their home departments and return to the traditional values of the expert model. Given this, we propose at the very least, that faculty are not penalized for participating in interdisciplinary collaboration. This requires, at a minimum, a systemic policy to not penalize faculty for participation and one that allows for renegotiations of faculty roles and departmental resources allocations as discussed in the structural chapter earlier in this book. In the scheme of academic work, this is a small change in the value system initially, but may be necessary to begin a culture of tolerance for interdisciplinary behaviors. As interdisciplinary behaviors become more successful on campus, perhaps the academic value system can be more receptive to the values of interdisciplinary collaboration.

In the end, improving the environment for interdisciplinary collaboration requires understanding the complex relationships that affect academic work, which includes a deep understanding of how disciplinary culture manifests itself regularly in most aspects of faculty life. A more systemic approach (Argyris & Schon, 1978; Senge, 1990) takes into account the interrelationships among the array of external, disciplinary, institutional, departmental, and individual factors influencing academic departments, faculty work, and priorities (Massey & Wilger, 1995), and activity such as interdisciplinary collaboration. Using an holistic approach to examine interdisciplinary collaboration's inclusion means looking at patterns of behavior, including their antecedents, attempting to assess implications of actions and trends. It allows us to examine not only the existence of interdisciplinary collaboration but, as importantly, to understand more clearly how various aspects of the environment (particularly disciplinary orientations and academic architectures) influence and interact to affect involvement in this form of scholarly engagement. A systems approach also allows us to develop synergistic understandings for how interdisciplinary collaboration might be more successfully integrated into the complexities of faculty work.

Without utilizing a more systemic or holistic approach to look for ways of accommodating interdisciplinary collaboration (and other forms of academic work), most change efforts are relegated to the individual level—a single faculty member involving herself in a collaborative activity with another faculty member from a different discipline. Certainly, this one-by-one approach is fine. It may reflect the ways in which faculty exercise control over their own work choices, and probably means that innovative academic work is more common than research findings would ever suggest. Yet, we argue that the opportunity for innovative faculty work, including interdisciplinary collaboration should be built into the university system rather than left only to the wherewithal of individual faculty who feel at liberty to take the perceived risk.

For example, university administrators and faculty leaders can influence an expanding academic culture to value interdisciplinary collaboration behaviors by using financial resources to encourage and reward faculty who participate in this work. Seeing such policies and practices reinforced by university administration and faculty leaders may foster more acceptance of interdisciplinary collaboration behaviors in faculty throughout the organization. The more faculty who participate in interdisciplinary collaboration are rewarded for it, the more support will be created for expanding the value system to complement the expert model. We believe this will be a long and probably heated process, but nothing encourages change like success. Like participating in interdisciplinary collaboration, changing the academic culture to include the values of interdisciplinary collaboration can be a risky adventure. And like most things of value, the outcomes are worth the risk. We believe interdisciplinary collaboration warrants the risk.

We want to quickly note that similar criticisms of the postsecondary system have already been made by those advocating the scholarship of teaching, the scholarship of engagement, outreach scholarship, and other less typical forms of faculty work as well (e.g., Boyer, 1990; Fear & Sandmann, 1997; Votruba, 1996). We see parallels between the methods of changing cultures to advance and support interdisciplinary collaboration and those required to promote outreach activity on college campuses. Advocates of reform in outreach scholarship such as Votruba (1996), Fear and Sandmann (1997), Ramaley (2000), and Zlotkowski (1998) do not suggest minor adjustments be made to the fringes of our academic cultures. Instead, they advocate a changed course and direction for the connected college and university of the future; they advocate a form of organizational change that expands the boundaries of acceptable scholarship and academic work. They argue for a postsecondary system that steps away from sole reliance on Stage One thinking.

LEADING THE LEARNING ORGANIZATION

Much of what we have come to understand about interdisciplinary collaboration, as noted, is wrapped up in the ideas of learning: learning at the individual faculty level how to embrace the disciplinary orientations of others and adopt the cultural lenses of these orientations for thinking differently about faculty work; learning at the group level how to move beyond coexistence and superficial knowledge engagement to becoming a cognitive team where the goal is synergy and generativity for each member; learning as a conceptualization of leadership that focuses on fostering others' cognitive processes in addition to the more "pedestrian" aspects of facilitating groups to accomplish a set of tasks; and learning as an organizational trait that leads to the potential for systemic change. In many ways, our interdisciplinary collaboration team then is a kind of learning organization, and the leadership can be seen as leading the learning organization.

There are many ways to characterize leaders of learning organizations and the kind of leadership required in these settings. Some of the labels that have become popular are designers, teachers, stewards (Senge, 1990), ringmasters, bridge specialists, boundary agents, and ombuds (Klein, 1990). The leader's focus broadens from strict attention on task completion to incorporating the value of facilitating learning in others. Even in an academic organization such as a research university, we are typically still predisposed to look for the charismatic, "out-front," traditional forms of leadership in our educational leaders. But we saw that different skills seem required when taking on the role of leading the interdisciplinary collaboration especially as it fully develops along the continua we described.

"Learning leaders" start with building the foundation of purpose and core values for the team, which we saw in the original vision of interdisciplinarity articulated by the project administrator of our research team.

Having this vision, she then helped stipulate some of the core values that would support an interdisciplinary collaboration, cultivating similar interests and visions in others. Although the goal of interdisciplinary collaboration was unique, the process of leadership early on was quite traditional. Having said that, we note quickly that the project administrator also provided opportunities for values, specific goals, and objectives to be developed by team members, thereby enhancing their ownership of the process.

Leaders of learning organizations continually work to understand the whole (Senge, 1990), which requires integrative thinking on their part. They also see the importance of fostering this way of thinking in team members. Leaders design learning processes for others (p. 345) so that each team member can come to see beyond their sphere of influence and expert knowledge. This way, the team sees the ways in which pieces fit together and how they need to adapt as ideas advance and change, rather than this being within the sight only of the leader. We saw instances of the project administrator of the team we studied trying to set up opportunities for learning among members as well as stepping out of the way when learning was taking place so as not to control it. She remained a central figure in the team's existence. Yet at the same time, by the end of our data collection period, she had relinquished daily responsibility for the team to the transition leader and other members were stepping up as intellectual leaders as well. They had not yet reached the "we did it ourselves" perspective that is often used to characterize the great learning facilitator-leader (Senge, 1990, Heider, 1989) but they were on their way to fully owning their processes.

In trying to stimulate learning processes of team members, the project administrator regularly had to ask tough questions of herself and of others, and encourage members to do the same. The learning processes involved kaleidoscope thinking where the means by which pieces of the organization, the disciplines, the project goal, and the community fit together were constantly questioned and reorganized as the team evolved (Kanter, 1999). Part of this learning process is connected to the intellectual neutral space we saw and other holding patterns (Bridges & Mitchell, 2000; Heifetz, 1994) from which members emerged with a more clear sense of direction, vision, and a collective perspective. It also involved developing high levels of trust and credibility within the team that were not based on authority and expertise. Rather, they came from listening, consistency, honor and respect of others' ideas and values, and building strong relationships (Bugay, 2001).

It was also clear to us that leaders of learning organizations are managers of meaning, who frame members' understandings of circumstances, issues, and so forth (Morgan, 1999). For the process to unfold, leaders have to get the mental models (Senge, 1990) or "habits of expectation" (Mezirow & Associates, 1990) of members on the table so that integrative learning and systems thinking can occur. Leaders help members restructure their views of reality to see beyond superficial conditions or events (and predispositions) to the underlying causes of problems and possibilities for resolution. Part of this process involves enabling dialogue to occur among members, setting aside disciplinary biases temporarily, and cultivating a common language through which members can find their individual and collective voices. As the project administrator described for us, this takes intellectual leadership.

In any learning process, one has to identify the underlying intellectual assumptions that derived, in our discussion, from faculty's disciplinary orientations. With the leader's help, members then need to critically assess assumptions, and reformulate them to permit development of a "more inclusive and permeable meaning perspective" (Mezirow, 1991, p. 155). Some of this we saw occurring through the introduction of intellectual neutral space and the emerging dialogue that followed. Common language can emerge and more integrated thinking begins. In a learning organization such as an interdisciplinary collaboration effort, the leader may still manage meaning in traditional ways to help members reach particular understandings. But more to the point, the leader manages, facilitates, and provides for the opportunities that support the learning transformations from which common understandings and common language can emerge. This is a somewhat different approach to managing meaning and one that requires a fundamentally different philosophy for the leader.

We raise this specific leadership point because of the important role common language played in solidifying our research team's collective experiences and because of the evidence it provided of cognitive team development. While common language may be an off-shoot of dialogue, we can also predict that many groups will not really reach this level of understanding. We certainly would not hold faculty to this achievement in Stage One organizational climates; the impetus for working this hard is totally lacking. Yet, for integrated learning to occur and transform members' thinking to allow for interdisciplinary collaboration, it is critical to move beyond the rhetoric of collegial conversation that avoids, or submerges, conflict. We are not suggesting differences do not exist or that disciplinary orientations no longer have a place in the discussion. But common language and dialogue embrace the differences rather than subvert them (Tierney, 1994). Leaders have to see the value in helping members reach a level of more genuine and deep understanding, and see their own role in this transition.

Learning leaders are stewards, which is often the most subtle role (Greenleaf, 1996; Senge, 1998). In many ways, the transition leader of our research team reflected this leadership philosophy in his approach to working for and with the team. Being an enabler of team activities, cultivating an environment that allowed members to do their best, attending to the developmental needs of members all are roles attributable to this definition of leadership. It primarily revolves around stewardship for the people and for the organization, which in the case of our research team was both the team itself and the community with which it was working.

Leading through the Dissonance

Leaders have to have an ability to build shared vision, bring to the surface and challenge prevailing mental models, and foster more systemic patterns of thinking. Leaders are responsible for learning, both at the individual and group levels. This learning starts with the principle of creative tension: seeing clearly where we want to be and telling us to trust where we are (Senge, 1990; Vaill, 1997; Weick, 2001). In our study, the real team vision emerged through the intellectual neutral space, although striving toward interdisciplinarity was always a dream of the project administrator. For some members of our research team, motivation to participate was a definition of the current state requiring their expert knowledge to fix what they viewed as "wrong."

However, fixing what is wrong is not creative tension, or even really learning (Argyris & Schon, 1978) because the deeper questions of process and substance (e.g., should we be doing this at all?) are never asked. To move away from "simply" problem solving to the learning anticipated in this project requires ripening of issues, finding holding patterns like intellectual neutral space, and the kind of adaptive work described by Heifetz (1994). It can be a period of painful adjustment, as we noticed in our research team. It is a risky proposition for the leader and for members, and involves elements of loss (Bridges & Mitchell, 2000). To learn and create adaptive solutions such as those that come from interdisciplinary collaboration, leaders ask members to "out and out give up something in the interests of something to be maintained, to be conserved, or to be gained. They may have to go through a period of refashioning loyalty ... or of feeling disloyalty to their own roots" (Heifetz & Linsky, 2002, p. 1). The values that helped faculty become successful in the expert model customary in academe are questioned by coming together in interdisciplinary collaborations (Heifetz & Laurie, 1997; Vaill, 1997). Yet, it is this expert knowledge base (technical ability, in Vaill's words, p. 12) that has to be suspended (not abandoned) and expressed differently so that, "room is created for the technical contributions of others." These are significant challenges to those socialized to particular disciplinary orientations and knowledge roles, and are experienced by team members and by the leaders themselves.

Leaders who opt to facilitate the adaptive work of integrated thinking characteristic of interdisciplinary collaboration will lead differently than we traditionally expect. They have to "get up on the balcony" (Heifetz, 1994; Heifetz & Laurie, 1997) to capture and reflect a holistic sense of the situation to group members, and to be able to see a different direction. This is not quite the same as visioning, heralded in traditional leadership research as the key to effective leadership. It does involve being able to move out of the fray and look across the multiple perspectives long enough to facilitate next steps. Leaders have to identify the adaptive challenges. They have to regulate the dissonance and maintain continued attention to the issues and tasks so that disciplinary clashes do not take over. They have to give the creative work and decision making to those directly involved, rather than holding out for a single end goal. So predicted outcomes will be uncommon. And leaders have to protect voices of those throughout the group (Heifetz & Laurie, 1997). We saw many of these intellectual leadership tasks played out by the project administrator of the research team we studied, and watched as the transition leader stepped in to try and enact this leadership role.

By assisting people to understand themselves and their world, it becomes possible to engage in the cognitive changes necessary to work beyond the disciplinary norms that typically characterize academic work. Yet, developing interdisciplinary collaboration as a form of learning organization is really a pattern of becoming (Senge, 1990, p. 345). As an intellectual configuration, it is not something to be arrived at but rather a continual renegotiation and integration of ideas and knowledge bases. In this interpretation, then, the leadership required to facilitate it is also ongoing. Because it is educative in that it involves individual and group learning, it is never done (Smyth, 1989; Vaill, 1997).

CONCLUDING THOUGHTS

The intellectual approach proposed for this project, while not entirely successful in creating a truly interdisciplinary experience, asked members to move beyond their personal research, inquiry, and academic preferences and to explore the utility of interdisciplinary work and multi-method scholarly engagement. For those who pursued their work in intellectual isolation, as they had "always done" research or outreach engagement, the experience was often frustrating, limiting, and did not produce their expected or intended results. For those willing to work beyond their disciplinary training and cognitive spheres, there was evidence of some degree of synergy, generativity, and a sense of collective pride in the outcome.

Bohen and Stiles (1998) suggest that faculty are motivated to participate in interdisciplinary collaborations because they desire to work with colleagues/scholars in related fields to create and explore new questions, to expand beyond the confines of their discipline, and because they have a genuine desire for intellectual discourse. It is an important strategy for addressing complex postsecondary problems and promoting institutional intellectual vitality.

Universities should capitalize on faculty motivations to work together and support consideration of interdisciplinary efforts. To do so, Bohen and Stiles (1998) make several stipulations. They assert that universities must: (1) promote interdisciplinary collaborative efforts that provide a clear vision of a compelling problem not solved by current structures and thus, requiring interdisciplinary applications; (2) promote leadership needed to bridge intellectual boundaries with the skills of an idea integrator, rapporteur, and fundraiser; (3) provide institutional commitment including administrative support, faculty leadership, physical space, stewardship to resolve tough issues (e.g., release time, incentives, administrative barriers), and new structures for the academic enterprise; (4) financial resources that allow the collaboration to act independently of other university structures; and (5) incentives and rewards for individual faculty participation in such collaboration (p. 46). Our research bore out many of the same ideas, and our recommendations are in consort with those of Bohen and Stiles.

We would add that universities need to eliminate any disincentives for participation and develop neutral spaces for interdisciplinary collaboration. There seems to be more writing on the intellectual engagement and learning processes of faculty around the act and art of teaching, then around the art and act of research and inquiry. If we can say it is a professionally moral obligation of faculty to engage in critical discourse and reflection about their teaching (Palmer, 1998; Smyth, 1989), it seems equally important to expect the same of those involved in research and inquiry. Yet, because of the emphasis on product rather than process in both arenas, we often abdicate the responsibilities without significant consequence to our prestige, reputations, and productivity. Academic leaders, governance committees, graduate preparation faculty, and faculty themselves need to address this disconnect if we are ever to see substantive change in the behavior of faculty and their commitment to this form of scholarly enterprise.

When we reflect on interdisciplinary collaboration as an intellectual process of engagement and a form of learning, different questions come to mind requiring different individual and institutional responses. One question becomes, if interdisciplinary collaboration can be a kind of borrowing of intellectual tools, and this appropriation is indeed learning, how do we effectively create the space and time in faculty work and faculty lives to support this ongoing cognitive process? If paradigm exploration, dialogue, and developing common language are prerequisites for integrative thinking, how do we prepare faculty to actively engage in these more time consuming activities that in some ways, negate their formal role as knowledge experts? If intellectual neutral space spawns "new" knowledge and creative responses to critical problems in education and society, how do we create or facilitate this ... or do we? In institutions known for their embedded cultures and slow change, how do we manipulate the kind of systemic reform that may be required to institutionalize this kind of academic and intellectual work, especially at a time when efficiency and accountability are more a part of societal rhetoric and government oversight than ever before? The answers are not easy nor are they necessarily generic across institutional settings. What appears clear, however, is that intellectual development through interdisciplinary collaboration is a fundamental change for knowledge engagement and faculty work.

In the end, interdisciplinary collaboration not only benefits society and constituent needs, it helps to fulfill institutional mission and values especially around the goal of knowledge creation and application. It also has important "internal" effects for faculty themselves in terms of revitalized teaching, new research opportunities, and overall intellectual vitality (Hirsch & Lynton, 1995). Interdisciplinary collaboration forces rejuvenation and regeneration among faculty, and thereby, provides some of the necessary churn within the academic system (Salter & Hearn, 1996). This churning of intellectual ideas is central to knowledge generation and the university enterprise so interdisciplinary collaboration can play a key role in organizational health and renewal. We conclude our study believing that interdisciplinary collaboration is truly an important form of organizational learning and transformation. Bringing this work to more prominent status in academic culture is key to promoting the scholarships of application and engagement, through better definitions and understandings, integration with and through teaching, research and service, and institutionalizing more effective evaluation mechanisms.

In closing, we realize we have come full circle from where we began this research project. Framing academic work as interdisciplinary collaboration is thinking out of the box. It provides faculty license to be original, creative, and to learn from and with each other. And that, we believe, is what knowledge creation and the mission of the modern university is all about.

APPENDIX

Research Design and Methodology

The data and analyses presented in this text were a result of an 18-month study of a university-community-agency partnership. The purpose of the project was to develop the community's capacity to own and operate a community center that would provide a wide range of services and respond to future needs of the community. The university team, which consisted of members from a number of disciplines, was contracted to provide technical assistance and training to an inner-city community council. The focus of this research was on the processes of interaction among the university team members who represented multiple disciplines. Members of the team were faculty, staff, and graduate students from five units at one university: social work, urban affairs, business, museum arts, and university outreach.

We examined the ways in which university team members developed and enacted an interdisciplinary team and the leadership issues associated with group cohesion. From this analysis, several themes emerged and an interdisciplinary collaboration model was developed to capture the complexity of the activity. Specifically, we examined the consequences for group processes, goal definition, and intervention strategies when competing paradigms exist, what leadership issues were present, and the degree of impact of university culture on successful interdisciplinary collaboration development.

A qualitative research design using grounded theory procedures and techniques was used (Strauss & Corbin, 1991). Data were collected through observations of team meetings, audio-recorded interviews with team members, analysis of project documents (i.e., minutes, memoranda, reports), and analysis of reflective papers written by team members that highlighted important decision points and other perceptions of group processes. The scope of the study was intended to include everything from the team's inception through the first 18 months of its project work. We were invited to assume research roles in studying the team's processes after work had already begun. Formal data collection began almost 11 months into the project and continued for another 7 months, although one of us began serving in an advisory capacity to the project administrator 6 months after the original project start date. At this time, all existing documents were compiled and independently reviewed by the research team members. Analyses were compared, initial codes generated, and preliminary themes developed. During this same period, we began attending team meetings as well, with at least one researcher attending regular meetings and compiling field notes. These meeting observations continued throughout the remainder of the project, a period of approximately 7 months.

Because neither of us were involved at the onset of the project, an attempt was made to generate a form of "baseline data." Each team member was asked to construct a reflective paper capturing their thoughts and observations about the team's processes since their initial involvement in the project. Members were asked to comment on their motivation for participation, their role in the project, group processes in early meetings, sources of conflict, conflict resolution, and group strategy development. Analyses of the project documents, reflective papers, and observation field notes were used in the development of an initial interview protocol. The protocol was pilot tested with one team member and revisions to wording and order of questions made accordingly. Face-to-face interviews were conducted over a 2-month period with a total of 9 of 10 team members, though all were invited to participate. Interviews were transcribed verbatim from audiotapes and field notes compiled for use in analysis.

Analysis of the reflective papers, group process observations, and verbatim interview transcripts were conducted through open coding to identify categories, concepts, and patterns (Patton, 1980; Strauss & Corbin, 1991). As in most qualitative research, analyses were ongoing throughout the data collection period. During the data collection process, each member of the research team independently analyzed the data sets. We met regularly during the concentrated data gathering period to discuss out observations, make preliminary coding categories and interpretations, and provide feedback into the data gathering and analyses processes.

This synergistic procedure is consistent with the evolving nature of the grounded theory approach (Strauss & Corbin, 1991). We attempted to document and analyze the emerging events of the group process in terms of how and why actions/interactions changed, remained unchanged, or regressed in relation to the project goals. Further, the process analyses sought to explain why planned actions or interactions broke down on the project, why problems emerged and why, in retrospect, the project produced growth and development, prematurely arrested, or failed in goal attainment. The extent to which we were successful in conducting these analyses was limited by the availability and nature of data collected and is described in more detail in the limitation section.

LIMITATIONS OF THE STUDY

There were a number of limitations to this study. The primary limitation was that this study of the team began 11 months into the overall project, due to various contract and research design issues. As a result, nearly 11 months of opportunity for observation and data gathering, primarily during the initial organizing and goal setting period were lost although again, one of us met regularly with the project administrator to debrief sessions, group events, and process issues. These meetings took place for almost 5 months before our official research study began. This period was also the time when the team membership and goal setting decisions were initially made. In an attempt to reconstruct this period, the study relied on written reflections from team members, interviews and document analysis as opposed to the preferred strategy of observation.

Another limitation was the absence of consistent documentation of many key activities such as the debriefing sessions that occurred after each training session where several team members assessed the success of each session and made decisions regarding modifications for the following sessions. These data could have been illustrative of team functioning and multidisciplinary growth and development. Much of the decision making regarding team activities and conflict resolution (i.e., budget or disciplinary approach) occurred over the phone or in private sessions of team subgroups where no documentation was probable, in spite of suggestions by the team leader that records be kept. This became particularly problematic for us when trying to track the change process (action-reaction-action) and team evolution through the various stages.

REFERENCES

Amey, M. J. (2002). Evaluating outreach performance. In C. L. Colbeck (Ed.), *Evaluating faculty performance—New Directions for Institutional Research* (No. 114, pp. 33-42). San Francisco: Jossey-Bass.

Argyris, C., & Schon, D. A. (1977). *Organizational learning: A theory of action perspective*. Reading, MA: Addison-Wesley.

Astin, A. W., & Astin, H. S. (Eds.). (2000). Principles of transformative leadership. In *Leadership reconsidered: Engaging higher education in social change.* (p. 8-17). W. K. Kellogg Foundation. Available: http://www.wkkf.org/pubs/CCT/Leader ship/Pub3368.pdf

Austin, A. E. (1990). Faculty cultures, faculty values. In W. G. Tierney (Ed.), *Assessing academic climates and cultures—New Directions in Institutional Research* (No. 68, pp. 61-74). San Francisco: Jossey-Bass.

Austin, A. E. (2002). Preparing the next generation of faculty: Graduate school as socialization to the academic career. *Journal of Higher Education, 73*(1), 94-122.

Austin, A. E., & Baldwin, R. G. (1991). *Faculty collaboration: Enhancing the quality of scholarship and teaching*. ASHE-ERIC Higher Education Report No. 7. Washington, DC: The George Washington University, School of Education and Human Development.

Austin, A. E., & Moore, K. M. (1997). *Realigning institutional missions and faculty work: A project on strategies and lessons*. East Lansing: Michigan State University.

Baldwin, R. G. (1990). Faculty career stages and implications for professional development. In J. H. Schuster & D. W. Wheeler (Eds.), *Enhancing faculty careers* (pp. 20-40). San Francisco: Jossey-Bass.

Baldwin, R. G., & Blackburn, R. T. (1981). The academic career as a developmental process. *Journal of Higher Education, 52*, 598-614.

Bartlett, K. T. (1990). Feminist legal methods. *Harvard Law Review, 103*, 829-888.

Baxter-Magolda, M. B (1992). *Knowing and reasoning in college: Gender-related patterns in students' intellectual development*. San Francisco: Jossey-Bass.

Becher, T. (1989). *Academic tribes and territories: Intellectual Enquiry and the Cultures of Disciplines*. Bristol, PA: The Society for Research into Higher Education and Open University Press.

Bennis, W. G. (1997). The secrets of great groups. *Leader to leader*, No. 3. The Peter F. Drucker Foundation for Nonprofit Management. Available: http://www. pfdf.org/leaderbooks/L2L/winter97/bennis.html

Bensimon, E. M., & Neumann, A. (1993) *Redesigning collegiate leadership: Teams and teamwork in higher education*. Baltimore: Johns Hopkins University Press.

Bergquist, W. H. (1992). *The four cultures of the academy: Insights and strategies for improving leadership in collegiate organizations*. San Francisco: Jossey-Bass.

Birnbaum, R. (1988). *How colleges work*. San Francisco: Jossey-Bass.

Blackburn, R. T., & Lawrence, J. H. 1995. *Faculty at work: Motivation, expectation, and satisfaction*. San Francisco: Jossey-Bass.

Bohen, S. J., & Stiles, J. (1998). Experimenting with models of faculty collaboration: Factors that promote their success. In S. H. Frost (Ed.), *Using teams in higher education: Cultural foundations for productive change—New Directions for Institutional Research* (No. 100, pp. 38-56). San Francisco: Jossey-Bass.

Boice, R. (1992). *The new faculty member: Supporting and fostering professional development*. San Francisco: Jossey-Bass.

Bolman, L. G., & Deal, T. E. (1997). *Reframing organizations: Artistry, choice and leadership* (2nd ed.). San Francisco: Jossey-Bass.

Bronstein, P., & Ramaley, J. A. (2002). Making the persuasive tenure case: Pitfalls and possibilities. In J. E. Cooper & D. D. Stevens (Eds.), *Tenure in the sacred grove: Issues and Strategies for women and minority faculty* (pp. 31-56). Albany, NY: State University of New York Press.

Boyer, E. (1990). *Scholarship reconsidered: Priorities of the professoriate*. Princeton, NJ: Carnegie Foundation for the Advancement of Teaching.

Bridges, W., & Mitchell, S. (2000). Leading transition: A new model for change. *Leader to leader*, No.16. The Peter F. Drucker Foundation for Nonprofit Management. http://www.pfdf.org/leaderbooks/L2L/spring2000/bridges. html

Bugay, D. P. (2001). *TransformActional leadership: Leaders building on trust*. International Leadership Association Proceedings. Academy of Leadership. http:// www.academy.umd.edu/ILA/2001proceedings/David.htm

Clark, B. R. (1963). *Faculty organization and authority*. Denver, CO: Western Interstate Commission for Higher Education.

Clark, B. R. (1987). *The academic life: Small Worlds, different worlds*. Princeton, NJ: Carnegie Foundation for the Advancement of Teaching.

Clark, S. M., & Corcoran, M. (1986). Perspectives on the professional socialization of women faculty: A case of accumulative disadvantage? *Journal of Higher Education, 57*(1), 20-43.

Colbeck, C. L. (1998). Merging in a seamless blend: How faculty integrate teaching and research. *Journal of Higher Education, 69*(6), 647-671.

Cronin, T. E. (1993). Reflections on leadership. In W. E. Rosenbach & R. L. Taylor (Eds.), *Contemporary issues in leadership* (3rd ed., pp. 7-25). Boulder, CO: Westview Press.

Cuoto, R. A. (2001). To give their gifts: The innovative, transforming leadership of adaptive work. In W. E. Rosenbach & R. L. Taylor (Eds.), *Contemporary issues in leadership* (5th ed., pp. 43-64). Boulder, CO: Westview Press.

DePree, M. (1998). Followership. In W. E. Rosenbach & R. L. Taylor (Eds.), *Contemporary issues in leadership* (4th ed., pp. 92-95). Boulder, CO: Westview Press.

Dill, D. D. (1982) The management of academic culture: Notes on the management of meaning and social integration. *Higher Education 11*, 303-320.

Doan, S. R. (1995). *The collaborative model: The effective model for the increasing interdependence of organizations*. ED 392 154.

Duryea, E. D. (1973). Evolution of university organization. In J. A. Perkins (Ed.), *The university as an organization*. Princeton, NJ: Carnegie Foundation for the Advancement of Teaching.

Ellis, N. E., & Joslin, A. W. (1990). *Gaining control of the pieces: Shared governance through collaboration*. Paper presented at the Southern Regional Council on Educational Administration Conference, Atlanta.

Engestrom, Y. (1999). Innovative learning in work teams: Analyzing cycles of knowledge creation in practice. In Y. Engestrom, R. Meittinen, & R.-J. Punamaki (Eds.), *Perspectives on activity theory* (pp. 377-404). Cambridge, England: Cambridge University Press.

Fairweather, J. S. (1988). *Entrepreneurship and Higher Education: Lessons for Colleges, Universities, and Industry*. ASHE-ERIC Higher Education Report No. 6. Washington, DC: Association for the Study of Higher Education.

Fairweather, J. S. (1993). Academic values and faculty rewards. *The Review of Higher Education, 17*(1), 43-68.

Fairweather, J. S. (1996). *Faculty work and public trust: Restoring the value of teaching and public service in American academic life*. Boston: Allyn & Bacon.

Fairweather, J. S. (2002). The mythologies of faculty productivity: Implications for institutional policy and decision making. *The Journal of Higher Education, 73*(1), 26-48.

Fay, B. (1987). *Critical social science: Liberation and its limits*. Ithaca, NY: Cornell University Press.

Fear, F. A., & Sandmann, L. R. (1997). Unpacking the service category: Reconceptualizing university outreach for the 21st century. *Continuing Higher Education Review, 59*(3), 117-122.

Forman, E. A., Minick, N., & Stone, C. A. (1993). *Contexts for learning: Sociocultural dynamics in children's development*. New York: Oxford University Press.

Foster-Fishman, P. G., & Stevens, D. D. (2002). Outreach in a new light: Documenting the scholarship of application. In J. E. Cooper & D. D. Stevens (Eds.), *Tenure in the sacred grove: Issues and strategies for women and minority faculty* (pp. 179-202). Albany, NY: State University of New York Press.

Gaff, J. G., Pruitt-Logan, A. S., Weibl, R. A., & Others. (2000). *Building the faculty we need: Colleges and universities working together*. Washington, DC: Association of American Colleges and Universities.

Giroux, H., & Freire, P. (1987). Series introduction. In D. Livingstone and contributors (Eds.), *Critical pedagogy and cultural power*. South Hadley, MA: Bergin & Garvey.

Glassick, C. E., Huber, M. T., & Maeroff, G. I. (1997). *Scholarship assessed: Evaluation of the professoriate*. San Francisco: Jossey-Bass.

Golde, C. M. (1998). Beginning graduate school: Explaining first-year doctoral attrition. In M. S. Anderson (Ed.), *The experience of being in graduate school: An exploration—New Directions for Higher Education, No. 101*. San Francisco: Jossey-Bass.

Gray, B. (1989). *Collaborating: Finding common ground for multi-party problems*. San Francisco: Jossey-Bass.

Greenleaf, R. K. (1996). *On becoming a servant-leader*. San Francisco: Jossey-Bass.

Greeno, J. G. (1997). On claims that answer the wrong question. *Educational Researcher, 26*(1), 5-17.

Gumport, P. J. (1991). Academic structure, culture, and the case of feminist scholarship. In M. C. Brown, Jr. (Ed.), *Organization and governance in higher education*. (5th ed., pp. 508-520). Boston: Pearson.

Harbert, A. S., Finnegan, D., & Tyler, N. (1997). Collaboration: A study of a children's initiative. *Administration in Social Work, 21*(3-4), 83-107.

Heider, R. (1989). The leader who knows how things happen. In W. E. Rosenbach & R. L. Taylor (Eds.), *Contemporary issues in leadership* (2nd ed., pp. 161-167). Boulder, CO: Westview Press.

Heifetz, R. A. (1994). *Leadership without easy answers*. Cambridge, MA: Harvard University Press.

Heifetz, R. A., & Laurie, D. L. (1997). The work of leadership. *Harvard Business Review, 75*(1), 124-134.

Heifetz, R. A., & Linsky, M. (2002). Leading with an open heart. Leader to Leader, No. 3. The Peter F. Drucker Foundation for Nonprofit Management. http://leadertoleader.org/leaderbooks/121/fall2002/heifetz.html

Helgesen, S. (1995). *The web of inclusion*. New York: Doubleday/Currency.

Hirsch, D., & Lynton, E. (1995). *Bridging two worlds: Professional service and service learning*. Boston: New England Resource Center for Higher Education, University of Massachusetts.

Jantsch, E. (1980). Interdisciplinarity: Dreams and reality. *Prospects: Quarterly Review of Education, 10*(3), 304-312.

Kanter, R. M. (1999). Enduring skills of change leaders. *Leader to leader*, No. 13. The Peter F. Drucker Foundation for Nonprofit Management. http://www.pfdf.org/leaderbooks/L2L/summer99/kanter.html

Kegan, R. (1982). *The evolving self: Problem and process in human development*. Cambridge, MA: Harvard University Press.

Kim, W. C., & Mauborgne, R. A. (1993). The wheel and the light. In W. E. Rosenbach & R. L. Taylor (Eds.), *Contemporary issues in leadership* (3rd ed., pp. 152-154). Boulder, CO: Westview Press.

Klein, J. T. (1990). *Interdisciplinarity: History, theory, and practice*. Detroit, MI: Wayne State University Press.

Kotter, J. P. (1996). *Leading change*. Boston: Harvard Business School Press.

Krasnow, M.H. (1997). *Learning to listen, talk, and trust: Constructing collaborations*. ED 408 540

Kuh, G. D., & Whitt, E. J. (1988). *The invisible tapestry: Culture in American colleges and universities.* ASHE-ERIC Higher Education Report No. 1. Washington, DC: Association for the Study of Higher Education.

Kuhnert, K. W., & Lewis, P. (1989). Transactional and transformational leadership: A constructive/developmental analysis. In W. E. Rosenbach & R. L. Taylor (Eds.), *Contemporary issues in leadership* (2nd ed., pp. 192-206). Boulder, CO: Westview Press.

Lattuca, L. R. (2002a). Learning interdisciplinarity: Sociocultural perspectives on academic work. *The Journal of Higher Education, 73*(6), 711-739.

Lattuca, L. R. (2002b). An overview of sociocultural and cultural historical perspectives. In E. Creamer (Chair), *Supporting new forms of collaborative faculty work.* Symposium presented at the Annual Meeting of the Association for the Study of Higher Education, Sacramento, CA.

Lave, J. (1997). The culture of acquisition and the practice of understanding. In D. Kirshner & J. A. Whitson (Eds.), *Situated cognition: Social, semiotic, and psychological perspectives* (pp. 17-35). Mahwah, NJ: Erlbaum.

Lave, J., & Wenger, E. (1991). *Situated learning: Legitimate peripheral participation.* New York: Cambridge University Press.

Licata, C. (1986). *Post-tenure faculty evaluation: Threat or opportunity?* ASHE-ERIC Higher Education Report No. 1. Washington, DC: Association for the Study of Higher Education.

Magolda, P. (2001). Border crossings: Collaboration struggles in education. *Journal of Educational Research, 96*(6), 346-358.

Masland, A. T. (1985). Organization culture in the study of higher education. *Review of Higher Education, 8,* 157-68.

Massey, W., & Wilger, A. (1995, July/August). Improving productivity: What faculty think about it and its effect on quality. *Change, 27*(4), 10-20.

Mattesich, P. W., & Monsey, B. R. (1992). *Collaboration: What makes it work?* St. Paul, MN: Amherst Wilder Foundation.

Menges, R. J., & Associates. (1999). *Faculty in new jobs: A guide to settling in, becoming established, and building institutional support.* San Francisco: Jossey-Bass.

Mezirow, J. (1991). *Transformative dimensions of adult learning.* San Francisco: Jossey-Bass.

Mezirow, J., & Associates. (1990). *Fostering critical reflection in adulthood: A guide to transformative and emancipatory learning.* San Francisco: Jossey-Bass.

Minick, N., Stone, C. A., & Forman, E. A. (1993). Introduction: Integration of individual, social, and institutional processes in accounts of children's learning and development. In E. A. Forman, N. Minick, & C. A. Stone (Eds.), *Contexts for learning: Sociocultural dynamics in children's development.* New York: Oxford University Press.

Mintzberg, H. (1979). *The structuring of organizations—A synthesis of the research.* Prentice-Hall.

Morgan, G. (1999). *Images of organizations* (2nd ed.). Beverly Hills, CA: Sage.

Neumann, A. (1999, April). *Passionate talk about passionate thought: The view from professors at early midcareer.* Paper presented at the Annual Meeting of the American Educational Education Association, Montreal.

Nyquist, J. D., Manning, L., Wulff, D. H., Austin, A. E., Sprague, J., Fraser, P. K., Calcagno, C., & Woodford, B. (May/June, 1999). On the road to becoming a professor: the graduate school experience. *Change*, 18-27.

O'Banion, T. (1997). *A learning college for the 21st century*. Phoenix, AZ: Oryx Press.

Oborn, C., & Shipley, G. L. (1995). *The university and the school: A leadership model for collaborative inquiry*. Research paper presented at the 1995 Annual Mid-Western Educational Research Association Conference, Chicago, IL. ED 398 224.

O'Looney, J. (1994). Modeling collaboration and social services integration: A single state's experience with developmental and non-developmental models. *Administration in Social Work, 18*(1), 61-86.

Organization for Economic Cooperation and Development. (1972). *Interdisciplinarity: Problems of teaching and research in universities*. Paris: OECD.

Palmer, P. J. (1998). *The courage to teach: Exploring the inner landscape of a teacher's life*. San Francisco: Jossey-Bass.

Patton, M. Q. (1980). *Qualitative evaluation methods*. Newbury Park, CA: Sage.

Ramaley, J. (2000). Embracing civic responsibility. *AAHE Bulletin, 52*(7), 9-13+.

Reynolds, A. (1992). Charting the changes in junior faculty: Relationships among socialization, acculturation, and gender. *Journal of Higher Education, 63*(6).

Rice, R. E. (1998). *Making a place for the new American scholar*. New Pathways Inquiry #1. Washington, DC: American Association for higher Education.

Rice, R. E., Sorcinelli, M. D., & Austin, A. E. (2000). *Heeding new voices: Academic careers for a new generation*. New Pathways Inquiry #7. Washington, DC: American Association of Higher Education.

Rogoff, B. (1990). *Apprenticeship in thinking: Cognitive development in social context*. New York: Oxford University Press.

Salter, L., & Hearn, A. (1996) *Outside the lines: Issues in interdisciplinary research*. Buffalo, NY: McGill-Queen's University Press.

Sandmann, L., & M. Flynn. 1997. *A model for neighborhood redevelopment through university-mediated intervention: Evaluation research plan*. Funding proposal. East Lansing, MI: Michigan State University.

Schein, E. (1985). *Organizational culture and leadership: A dynamic view*. San Francisco: Jossey-Bass.

Scott, W. R. (2002). *Organizations: Rational, natural, and open systems* (5th ed.). Englewood Cliffs, NJ: Prentice-Hall.

Senge, P. M. (1990). *The fifth discipline: The art and practice of the learning organization*. New York. Doubleday.

Senge, P. M. (1996). The ecology of leadership. *Leader to leader,* No. 2. The Peter F. Drucker Foundation for Nonprofit Management. http://www.pfdf.org/leader books/L2L/fall96/senge.html

Senge, P. (1998). Leading learning organizations. In W. E. Rosenbach & R. L. Taylor (Eds.), *Contemporary issues in leadership* (4th ed., pp. 174-178). Boulder, CO: Westview Press.

Smyth, J. (1989). A "pedagogical" and "educative" view of leadership. In J. Smyth, (Ed.), *Critical perspectives on educational leadership* (pp. 179-204). New York: The Falmer Press.

Strauss, A., & Corbin, J. (1991). *Basics of qualitative research: Grounded theory procedures and techniques*. Newbury Park, CA: Sage.

Tierney, W. G. (1989). *Curricular landscapes, democratic vistas: Transformative leadership in higher education*. Westport, CT: Praeger.

Tierney, W. G. (1991). Organizational culture in higher education: Defining the essentials. In M. Peterson (Ed.), *ASHE Reader in Organization and Governance in Higher Education* (pp. 126-139). Lexington, MS: Ginn Press.

Tierney, W. G. (1994). *Building communities of difference: Higher education in the twenty-first century*. Baltimore: Johns Hopkins University Press.

Tierney, W. G. (1999). *Building the responsive campus: Creating high performance colleges and universities*. Baltimore: Johns Hopkins University Press.

Tierney, W. G., & Bensimon, E. M. (1996). *Promotion and tenure: Community and socialization in academe*. Albany, NY: SUNY Press.

Trower, C. A., Austin, A. E., & Sorcinelli, M. D. (2001, May) Paradise lost. *AAHE Bulletin*. http://www.aahebulletin.com/public/archive/paradiselost.asp

Tjosvold, D. (1986). The dynamics of interdependence in organizations. *Human Relations 39,* 517-540.

Trubowitz, S. L., & Longo, P. (1997). *How it works—Inside a school-college collaboration*. New York: Teachers College Press.

Tuckman, B. W. (1965). Developmental sequence in small groups. *Psychological Bulletin, (63)*6, 384-389.

Vaill, P. B. (1997). The learning challenges of leadership. In *The balance of leadership and followership working papers*. Kellogg Leadership Studies Project. College Park, MD: Academy of Leadership Press.

Votruba, J. C. (1996). Strengthening the university's alignment with society challenges and strategies. *Journal of Public Service and Outreach, 1*(1), 29-36.

Wertsch, J. V. (1985). *Vygotsky and the social formation of the mind*. Cambridge, MA: Harvard University Press.

Wertsch, J. V., del Rio, P., & Alvarez, A. (Eds.). (1995). Sociocultural studies: History, action, and mediation. In *Sociocultural studies of the mind* (pp. 1-34). New York: Cambridge University Press.

Weick, K. (2001). Leadership as the legitimation of doubt. In W. Bennis, G. M. Spreitzer, & T. G. Cummings (Eds.), *The future of leadership: Today's top leadership thinkers speak to tomorrow's leaders* (pp. 91-102).San Francisco: Jossey-Bass.

Weiland, S. (1994). Writing the academic life: Faculty careers in narrative perspective. *Review of Higher Education, 17,* 395-422.

Zlotkowski, E. (Ed.). (1998). *Successful service learning programs: New models of excellence in higher education*. Bolton, MA: Anker.

AUTHOR INDEX

SUBJECT INDEX